Praise for Alister McGrath's C. S. LEWIS – A LIFE

To the question of whether the world really needs another biography of C. S. Lewis, McGrath's lucid and unsentimental portrait of the Christian champion responds with a resounding 'yes.' The year 2013 marks the 50th anniversary of Lewis's death, and times have changed and evangelical sentiments have matured. McGrath offers a new and at times shocking look into the complicated life of this complex figure, in a deeply researched biography. The author takes us headlong into the heart of a Lewis we've known little about: his unconventional affair with Mrs. Jane Moore; his hostile and deceptive relationship with his father; his curiosity about the sensuality of cruelty. McGrath navigates the reader through these messy themes, ultimately landing us onto the solid ground of Lewis's postconversion legacy. He shows with skill, sympathy, dispassion, and engaging prose that Lewis, like the rest of us, did the best he could with the hand he was dealt. But he got over it, as must all those who would prefer a Lewis without shadows.

– *Publishers Weekly*, starred review

This biography is the one Lewis's admirers – especially those who, like him, believe that books are to be read and enjoyed – should prefer to all others.

– *Booklist*, starred review

This fine, donnish biography concentrates on presenting a broadly sympathetic view of the man, the Christian apologist, and the scholar. Alister McGrath read Lewis's writings in order of their composition, which lends him insight into their deeper structures, particularly with regard to his joyous conversion to Christianity (apparently on a journey to Whipsnade Zoo) and his in-depth understanding of medieval literature and imagery. McGrath is a clear-eyed, learned companion . . .

This is a finely balanced book, which allows Lewis's works to speak for themselves without drawing crude parallels with his life, something that Lewis himself would have admired. And it leaves the reader marvelling at the joy and wonder that inhabit the Narnia books: that enchanted glimpse into something beautiful and eternal.

– Philip Womack, *The Telegraph*

A thoughtful, erudite lit-crit appraisal of the writings, plus an unabashed serenade for Lewis's theology.

– Peter Stanford, *The Guardian*

Alister McGrath gives us much food for thought in this dutiful, sound and worthy book.

– Paul Johnson, *The Spectator*

There have been plenty of biographies of Lewis – I once wrote one myself –but I do not think there has been a better one than Alister McGrath's.

– A. N. Wilson

Many of us thought we knew most of what there was to know about C. S. Lewis. Alister McGrath's new biography makes use of archives and other material that clarify, deepen and further explain the many sides of one of Christianity's most remarkable apologists. This is a penetrating and illuminating study.

– N. T. Wright

A welcome addition to the biographical literature on C. S. Lewis, which includes several valuable new perspectives. McGrath's book will gain a permanent position in Lewis scholarship for his brilliant and, to my mind, undeniable re-dating of Lewis's conversion to Theism. How we all missed this for so long is astonishing!

– Michael Ward, author of *Planet Narnia*

Alister McGrath's new biography of C. S. Lewis is excellent. It's filled with information based on extensive scholarship but is nonetheless extremely readable. It not only devotes great attention to the formation and character of Lewis the man, it offers incisive and balanced analyses of all his main literary works. Lewis's impact on me was profound and lasting, and Dr McGrath clearly explains why so many believers and Christian leaders today would say the same thing.

– Timothy Keller

Alister McGrath sheds new light on the incomparable C. S. Lewis. This is an important book.

– Eric Metaxas, author of *Bonhoeffer*

ALISTER McGRATH

Deep Magic, Dragons and Talking Mice

How Reading C.S. Lewis Can Change Your Life

HODDER &
STOUGHTON

First published in Great Britain in 2014 by Hodder & Stoughton
An Hachette UK company

1

First published as *If I had lunch with Lewis* by Tyndale House Publishers, Inc.
The Chronicles of Narnia, Narnia, and all book titles, characters, and
locales original to The Chronicles of Narnia are trademarks of
C. S. Lewis (PTE.) Ltd. Use without permission is strictly prohibited.
The Lion, the Witch and the Wardrobe is a trademark of C. S. Lewis (PTE.) Ltd.

A CIP catalogue record for this title is available from the British Library

ISBN 978 1 444 75030 0
Trade Paperback ISBN 978 1 444 75031 7
eBook ISBN 978 1 444 75032 4

Typeset in Plantin Light by Hewer Text UK Ltd, Edinburgh

Printed and bound in the UK by CPI Group (UK) Ltd, Croydon CR0 4YY

Hodder & Stoughton policy is to use papers that are natural, renewable
and recyclable products and made from wood grown in sustainable
forests. The logging and manufacturing processes are expected to
conform to the environmental regulations of the country of origin.

Hodder & Stoughton Ltd
338 Euston Road
London NW1 3BH

www.hodderfaith.com

CONTENTS

PREFACE

C.S. Lewis is one of the best-known writers of the twentieth century. Big-budget films of his Narnia novels have brought his books to a new, worldwide audience. Yet Lewis was famous long before the films came along. In his day, he was celebrated as one of the world's experts on English literature. His lectures at Oxford and Cambridge were packed out with eager students, who hung on his every word.

Lewis is now remembered mainly for two things. First, he is revered as the author of the seven novels which make up the Chronicles of Narnia. These books – especially their showcase opener, *The Lion, the Witch and the Wardrobe* – have become classics of English literature. The Narnia books bring home the power of well-told stories to captivate the imagination and open up some of the biggest questions of human existence – such as how we become good people and how we discover the meaning of life. They draw us into a rich, imaginative world, which helps us to think through the big questions of meaning and value in our own.

The second thing for which Lewis is now remembered is his Christian writing. Lewis was an angry atheist in his youth. He served in the British army during the First World War, and gave up on religion because of the suffering and destruction he saw around him. However, over a period of years he reconsidered his position and gradually came to the view that belief in God was the most satisfying way of looking at things. Lewis explained his change of heart in a series of best-selling books, most notably *Mere Christianity*.

Although Lewis is best known as a writer, we must never forget that his life was complex, difficult and occasionally tragic. His mother died of cancer before Lewis was ten years old. He fought on the battlefields of France during the First World War and was seriously wounded in combat. He married late in life, only to suffer tragedy as his wife slowly lost her long fight against cancer. Lewis is a rare example of someone who had to think about life's great questions because they were forced on him by his own experiences. Lewis is no armchair philosopher. His ideas were forged in the heat of suffering and despair.

So why this book? How can C.S. Lewis – who is best known for his Narnia novels – help us to think about the meaning of life? The idea for this book came while I was talking to a group of students in Oxford about Lewis. I wanted to explore some themes in his writings – such as his rich and rewarding idea of 'Joy'. The students, however, had very different ideas. They wanted to learn *from* Lewis, not learn *about* him. Lewis was a big name, a role model. They wanted to know what Lewis thought about the big questions of life. This, they told me, would help them sort themselves out. It sounded like a good idea. So we began to look at what Lewis had to say about the meaning of life. And this approach worked.

We all want to learn from people who have shown themselves to be thoughtful and helpful in dealing with the big questions of life. That's why so many of us turn to close friends or trusted colleagues and ask if we can have some time with them to get their advice. 'Let's have lunch!' is not a suggestion that we just eat food; it's a request to spend time together, to get to know people better and talk things through. We want to listen to those who have been through difficult situations like the ones we're now facing, and learn how they coped with them. We want them to tell us how they made sense of things so that we can do the same.

That's why so many people try to find 'mentors' – older and wiser people who can pass on their wisdom and help us by their example and encouragement. Or 'critical friends' – people who are on our side but are still willing to say difficult things to help us move on. Or 'life coaches' – people who help us achieve our goals. These are people we trust and respect, who can walk alongside us and help us move on in life and get more out of it. They are not just knowledgeable. They are something more important than that. They are *wise*.

It's like that party game people sometimes play, in which they're asked to name three people they would like to have lunch with. Who would the guests be? And why? What would the people hope to talk about? I'd like to have lunch with C.S. Lewis – and so would most of the people I know! It would be wonderful to sit down and discuss the greatest questions of life with him over some food and drink. After all, as Lewis himself pointed out, there are few greater pleasures than sharing food, drink and companionship. See this book as my invitation to you, my reader, to sit down with Lewis and me in some quiet place to think about some of the persistent questions and dilemmas every human being faces in this life.

Lewis is one of a very small group of people who both learned from life's challenges and was able to pass his wisdom on, elegantly and effectively. That's why the sales of Lewis's books today are greater than at any point during his lifetime. He is clearly someone whom many regard as helpful, informative and reflective. So why not see him as a mentor, coach or critical friend? Lewis's writings show that he was more than willing to act in these roles to his friends. His vast correspondence, for example, regularly provided advice and wisdom to both close friends and relative strangers. His *Screwtape Letters* (1942) is one of the most original works of spiritual direction ever written.

This work is a series of imagined conversations with Lewis. We could think of them as lunches at a local Oxford pub. Or perhaps as tutorials, in which some of the great questions of life are opened up for discussion and debate. What would Lewis say to someone trying to cope with grief? Or someone wondering how best to explain the Christian faith to an atheist friend? Or someone wanting to be a better person, or worried that his or her faith might be something make-believe, invented to cope with the harshness of life? Thanks to Lewis's own writings and the huge literature about Lewis, we know the sorts of things that he would say to people asking those questions. And that's what this book is all about: letting Lewis help us as we wrestle with questions and try to become better people. Of course, as we'll find out, Lewis has some questions of his own that we must consider as well.

Anyone who has seen the film *Shadowlands* might wonder if having lunch with Lewis – however imaginary! – would be much fun. Anthony Hopkins portrays Lewis as a solemn, pompous and rather tedious person who would probably bore his lunch companions to death. Happily, the real C.S. Lewis was nothing like that. His friends – such as George Sayer – fondly remember Lewis as a witty person with a 'glorious sense of humour' and a 'rather boyish sense of fun'. He was a 'joy to meet' and a 'wonderful companion'. Lunch with Lewis would have been a treat. He would have dispensed wisdom with laughter and good humour.

Lewis's ideas are often wise and worth listening to, but that doesn't mean we must agree with everything he says. I once had to attend a course on management at Oxford University. At the time, I held a senior position in the university which had managerial responsibilities. The course was intended to help me and other colleagues deal with these challenges more effectively. I remember one of those lectures vividly. It was about choosing friends who would help us make the best decisions.

'Don't surround yourself with clones of yourself,' we were told. 'Talk to people you really respect – even if they disagree with you.' Such people may not agree with you on everything, but they will present you with options that you know you have to take seriously. Your final decisions will be much better, because you will have been forced to think about possibilities you might not agree with but which might turn out to be right.

That's the spirit in which this book was conceived and written. Lewis will be our conversation partner. That doesn't mean he is right about everything. It just means he is someone really worth listening to. Lewis is a profoundly interesting and worthwhile person whom we know we have to take seriously, even if we end up disagreeing with him.

Lewis died in 1963. So how can we listen to him? One way might be to invent some imaginary dialogue, putting words into Lewis's mouth. But that's not fair, either to Lewis or to my readers. It's far better to provide accurate summaries of Lewis's ideas, spiced up with some of his better phrases and quotes, to draw readers into his way of thinking. We will explore his ideas, see how they might work and figure out how we might use them.

Let's pretend that we plan to meet Lewis regularly to talk about things. We will use a pattern suggested by the structure of academic terms at both of Lewis's universities, Oxford and Cambridge. Each university has three teaching terms of eight weeks. Lewis's working life was organised around these eight-week blocks of time. So let's pretend we are going to meet Lewis once a week during one of these terms. We might meet in one of Lewis's favourite watering holes in Oxford – such as The Eagle and Child or its close neighbour The Lamb and Flag. Or we might be more adventurous, following the walks that Lewis so loved along the river through Port Meadow to village pubs – such as The Perch at Binsey or The Trout at Wolvercote. And as we walk, we can talk about some of life's big questions.

Each of these eight conversations brings together more or less the same elements. We will learn part of Lewis's story, allowing us to understand how a particular question or concern became important to him. (For a more complete look at Lewis's life, see 'Introducing Lewis' on pages 185–94.) Then we'll look at how he responded to the question or concern. What did he do? What did he think? Sometimes we'll listen to Lewis's own words; sometimes I will paraphrase him or draw out his meaning using analogies or ideas that he didn't himself use but which help us to see what he's getting at. Finally, we'll work out how we might be able to use what we've learned for our benefit. How might his advice affect the way we think, or the way we live?

It always helps to have a major thinker like Lewis introduced by someone who knows his writings and ideas really well and can help you make sense of them. I've been reading Lewis for the last forty years and have come to appreciate his wisdom at many levels, as well as working out how best to explain and apply his ideas. But in the end, you need to read Lewis himself. Lewis has an elegant, winsome and engaging style that virtually none of his commentators – and certainly not I! – can imitate.

You could see this work as a preface to reading Lewis, just as Lewis once wrote a superb preface to the reading of John Milton's classic *Paradise Lost*. For this reason, the Further Reading section (pages 175–83) makes very specific suggestions about which of Lewis's writings you might like to read if you want to follow through on the themes found in this book, as well as other works that might help you take things further. The editions used are noted at the end of this work. I'll also provide you with details of some books about Lewis that will help you get more out of reading him.

So where shall we start? There's little doubt where Lewis would like us to begin – with his discovery of Christianity, which quickly became the moral and intellectual compass of his world. So let's begin by asking Lewis about the meaning of life.

Alister McGrath
London, September 2013

The Grand Panorama: C.S. Lewis on the Meaning of Life

I believe in Christianity as I believe that the Sun has risen, not only because I see it, but because by it I see everything else.

C.S. Lewis, 'Is Theology Poetry?'

It's easy to imagine arriving for our first meeting with Lewis with questions buzzing through our heads, not knowing quite what to ask first. But perhaps the first thing Lewis might emphasise is that meaning matters.

Maybe Lewis would have thumped the lunch table to emphasise his point, causing the crockery to shudder. We might be taken aback. Weren't we the ones meant to be asking the questions? Yet Lewis is challenging *us*! Perhaps that's because he realised how important it is to sort this out as a first order of business. We all need to build our lives on something that is stable, solid and secure. And until we find this foundation, we can't really begin to live properly. To use a distinction that Lewis teased out in *Mere*

Christianity, there's a big difference between just *existing* and really *living*.

So why does meaning matter?

Human beings are meaning-seeking creatures. Deep down within all of us is a longing to work out what life is all about and what we're meant to be doing. Whether it's the university student wondering what subject to study or the Christian seeking God's will or the armchair philosopher contemplating his or her purpose in the world, most of us want a reliable foundation for our lives and are asking questions that relate to it. Why am I alive? What is this life about? What is at life's core? What is my relationship to the physical world and the others around me? Is there a God, and what difference does it make?

We all need a lens through which to look at reality and make sense of it. Otherwise we are overwhelmed by it. The poet T.S. Eliot made this point in one of his poems. Humanity, he remarked, 'cannot bear very much reality'. We need a way of focusing it or weaving its threads together to disclose a pattern. Otherwise everything looks chaotic – blurred, out of focus and meaningless.

The French atheist philosopher Jean-Paul Sartre, who shaped the thinking of many bright young things in the 1960s, saw life as pointless: 'Here we sit, all of us, eating and drinking to preserve our precious existence and really there is nothing, nothing, absolutely no reason for existing.'[1] Yet it's hard to live in a meaningless world. What's the point?

Realising that there is meaning and purpose in life keeps us going in times of perplexity and difficulty. This point was underscored by Viktor Frankl, whose experiences in Nazi concentration camps during the Second World War showed the importance of discerning meaning in traumatic situations.[2] Frankl realised that someone's chance of survival depended on a will to live, which in turn depended on being able to find meaning and purpose in hopeless situations. Those who coped best with apparently hopeless situations were those with 'frameworks of meaning'. These allowed them to make sense of their experiences.

Frankl argued that if we can't make sense of events and situations, we are unable to cope with reality. He quoted from the German philosopher Friedrich Nietzsche: the person 'who has a why to live for can bear with almost any how'. We need a mental map of reality that allows us to position ourselves, helping us to find our way along the road of life. We need a lens which brings into focus the fundamental questions about human nature, the world and God.

Recent studies of trauma have emphasised the importance of sustaining a 'sense of coherence'[3] as a means of coping with seemingly senseless or irrational events, particularly those which involve suffering.[4] In other words, those who cope best are those who can see beneath the surface of an apparently random and pointless world and grasp the deeper structure of reality. The great Harvard psychologist William James pointed out many years ago that this is what religious faith is all about. According to James, we need to have 'faith in the existence of an unseen order of some kind in which the riddles of the natural order may be found and explained'.[5]

Of course, some would argue that any quest for meaning is simply misguided. There is nothing to find, so there is no point in looking. Richard Dawkins, who modestly declares himself to be the world's most famous and respected atheist, insists that the universe has 'no design, no purpose, no evil and no good, nothing but blind, pitiless indifference'.[6] We may invent meaning to console ourselves, but there is no 'bigger picture'. It's all a delusion, something we have made up.

I took that view myself in my late teens. I thought people who believed in God were mad, bad, or sad. I was better than that! Atheism was an act of rebellion, an assertion of my right to believe whatever I liked. Admittedly, it was a little dull. But who cared about that? It may have been austere to the point of being dreary, but it was right! The fact that it did nothing for me was proof that I had adopted it because of its truth, not its attractiveness or relevance. Yet a tiny voice within me whispered, *Are things* really *that simple? What if there is more to life than this?*

Lewis did not help me break free from this dull and lifeless worldview. Yet as I began to read Lewis from about 1974 on, he did help me in one very important way. Lewis enabled me to name what I had found wrong with atheism. He helped me to put a jumble of insights and intuitions into words. And as I struggled to find my feet and my bearings in the Christian world, he quickly became my unofficial mentor. I had never met him, yet his words and wisdom became – and have remained – important to me. I would love to have met Lewis – over lunch, or a drink, or in a tutorial – not so much to bombard him with questions, but simply to thank him for helping me grow in my faith.

It's time to bring C.S. Lewis into the conversation. Lewis was an atheist as a young man, yet he gradually realised that atheism was intellectually vulnerable and existentially unsatisfying. Let's find out why. Let's imagine that a group of us are having lunch with Lewis, and one of us asks him how he came to find meaning in life – or, specifically for him, how he became a Christian. What might he say?

Lewis's Doubts about His 'Glib and Shallow Rationalism'

Lewis was a convinced atheist by the age of sixteen. He was quite clear that religion had been explained away by the leading scholars of the 1910s. All the best scholarship of the day had shown that religion was just a primitive human instinct. This scholarship seemed to say, 'We've grown up now and don't need this.' Nobody could take belief in God seriously any more.

His views were hardened by the suffering and violence he witnessed while serving in the trenches in the First World War. Lewis had trained in an officer-cadet battalion in Oxford during the summer of 1917 before being commissioned as an officer in the Somerset Light

Infantry and posted to northern France. The suffering and destruction he saw around him convinced him of the pointlessness of life and the non-existence of God.

Lewis's experiences during the First World War made him angry with God – even though he believed that there was no God to be angry with. Like so many disillusioned and cynical young men, Lewis wanted someone to hate, someone to blame for the ills of the world. And, like so many before and after him, Lewis blamed God for everything. How dare God create him without his permission![7] But his atheism did not provide him with a 'framework of meaning' that made any sense of the devastation and anguish caused by the war. And he had to face up to the awkward fact that, if there was no God, blame for the war's horrors had to be laid firmly on human beings. Lewis seems gradually to have realised that the violence and brutality of the war raised troubling questions about a godless humanism as much as it did about Christianity. His 'grim and deadly' atheism did not make much sense of his wartime trauma, let alone help him to cope with it.[8]

The literature concerning the Great War and its aftermath emphasises the physical and psychological damage it wreaked on soldiers at the time and on their return home. The irrationality of the war called into question whether there was any meaning in the universe or in individual existence. Many students returning to study at Oxford after the war experienced considerable difficulty adjusting to normal life, which led to frequent nervous breakdowns.

Lewis himself hardly ever mentions the Great War. He seems to have 'partitioned' or 'compartmentalised' his life as a way of retaining his sanity. Literature – above all, poetry – became Lewis's firewall. It allowed him to keep the chaotic and meaningless external world at a safe distance and shielded him from the existential devastation it wreaked on others.

Lewis's continuing commitment to atheism in the 1920s was grounded in his belief that it was *right*, a 'wholesome severity',[9] even though he admitted that it offered a 'grim and meaningless' view of life. He took the view that atheism's intellectual rectitude trumped its emotional and existential inadequacy. Lewis did not regard atheism as liberating or exciting; he seems simply to have accepted it, without enthusiasm, as the thinking person's only intellectual option – a default position, without any particular virtues or graces.

Yet during the 1920s, Lewis reconsidered his attitude towards Christianity. The story of his return to the faith he had abandoned as a boy is described in great detail in his autobiography, *Surprised by Joy*. After wrestling with the clues concerning God that he found in human reason and experience, he eventually decided that intellectual honesty compelled him to believe and trust in God. He did not want to; he felt, however, that he had no choice.

In *Surprised by Joy*, Lewis tells us how he experienced the gradual approach of God. It was, he suggests, like a game of chess. Every move he made to defend himself was countered by a better move on God's part. His arguments against faith seemed increasingly inadequate and unconvincing. Finally, he felt he had no option but to give in and admit that God was God, becoming the 'most dejected and reluctant convert in all England'.

So what made Lewis change his mind? How did a hardened, dogmatic atheist become one of the greatest apologists for Christianity of the twentieth century and beyond? And what can we learn from this? Let's begin by looking at how Lewis's disenchantment with atheism began, and where it took him.

There are clear signs that Lewis began to become disenchanted with atheism in the early 1920s. For a start, it was imaginatively uninteresting. Lewis began to realise that atheism did not – and could not – satisfy the deepest longings of his heart or his intuition that there was more to life than what was seen on the surface. Lewis put it this way in a famous passage from *Surprised by Joy*:

> On the one side, a many-islanded sea of poetry and myth; on the other, a glib and shallow rationalism. Nearly all that I loved I believed to be imaginary; nearly all that I believed to be real I thought grim and meaningless.[10]

So what did Lewis mean by this? For a start, Lewis was putting into words his growing dissatisfaction with the simplistic account of things offered by atheism. His 'glib and shallow rationalism' dismissed the deep questions of life, offering only superficial responses. Atheism was existentially insignificant, having nothing to say about the deepest questions of the human mind or the yearnings of the human heart. We can prove shallow, superficial and unimportant things. But the things that really matter – the truths by which we live, whether they are political, moral, or religious – simply cannot be proved in this way.

Lewis began to realise that he had allowed himself to be trapped inside some kind of rationalist cage or prison. He had limited reality to what reason alone could prove. And as he came to realise, reason couldn't even prove its own trustworthiness. Why not? Because we would then be using reason to judge reason. Human reason would be both judge and defendant! As Lewis later put it, 'Unless the measuring rod is independent of the things measured, we can do no measuring.'[11]

But what if there was something *beyond* the scope of human reason? And what if this greater world dropped hints of its existence into our own world? What if an archer from that greater world were to shoot arrows into ours, alerting us to its existence? Lewis began to think that the world around us and our own experiences were full of 'clues' to the meaning of the universe.

Gradually, Lewis came to realise that these hints and clues pointed to a world beyond the frontiers of reason. We may hear snatches of its music in the quiet moments of life. Or sense its fragrance wafted towards us by a gentle breeze on a cool evening. Or hear stories of others who have discovered this land and are ready to share their adventures. All these 'signals of transcendence' – to borrow a phrase from the American sociologist Peter

Berger – help us to realise that there is more to existence than our everyday experience. As the great British apologist G.K. Chesterton (who was much admired by Lewis) pointed out long ago, the human imagination reaches beyond the limits of reason to find its true object. 'Every true artist', he argued, feels 'that he is touching transcendental truths; that his images are shadows of things seen through the veil.'[12]

The Importance of our Intuitions

Alongside Lewis the cool-headed thinker we find a very different style of thinker – someone who was aware of the power of the human imagination and the implications of this power for our understanding of reality. Perhaps one of the most original aspects of Lewis's writing is his persistent and powerful appeal to the religious imagination. Lewis was aware of certain deep human emotions and intuitions that seemed to point to a rich and enriching dimension of our existence beyond time and space. There is, Lewis suggested, a deep and intense feeling of longing within human beings which no earthly object or experience can satisfy. Lewis named this sense 'Joy' and argued that it pointed to God as its ultimate source and goal. God shoots 'arrows of joy' into our hearts to awaken us from a simplistic atheism and lazy agnosticism, and to help us find our way home.

Lewis explored this further in a remarkable wartime sermon, preached at Oxford in June 1941, titled 'The Weight of Glory'. Lewis spoke of 'a desire which no natural happiness will satisfy', 'a desire, still wandering and uncertain of its object and still largely unable to see that object in the direction where it really lies'. There is something self-defeating about human desire, he remarks, in that what is desired, when it is actually achieved, seems to leave that desire unsatisfied. Lewis illustrates this from the age-old quest for beauty. 'The books or the music in which we thought the beauty was located will betray us if we trust to them; it was not *in* them, it only came *through* them, and what came through them was longing.'[13] Human desire, the deep and bittersweet longing for something that will satisfy us, points *beyond* finite objects and finite persons (who seem able to fulfil this desire yet eventually prove incapable of doing so). Our sense of desire points *through* these objects and points persons towards their real goal and fulfilment in God.

Atheism had to dismiss such feelings and intuitions as deluded nonsense. For a while, Lewis went along with this. Then he realised that it was ridiculous. He was locked into a way of seeing things that prevented him from appreciating their true significance. Lewis began to trust his intuitions and explore where they led him. There was, he realised, a 'big picture' that made sense of life. It was called Christianity.

A 'Big Picture': Seeing Things in a New Way

In our conversations, Lewis would be sure to drop in some wonderful statements we would take away and relish, turning them over in our minds to make sure we had fully appreciated their depth and brilliance. Here's one he might have thrown into the conversation: 'I believe in Christianity as I believe that the Sun has risen, not only because I see it, but because by it I see everything else.'[14]

What is Lewis getting at here? Basically, he is putting into words one of the most fundamental reasons he became a Christian. The Christian faith, Lewis discovered, gave him a lens that brought things into focus. It was like turning on a light and seeing things properly for the first time. The powerful image of the sun rising and illuminating a dark landscape properly summed up Lewis's basic conviction that Christianity makes sense of things – far more sense than his earlier atheism.

Lewis came to realise that truth is about seeing things rightly, grasping their deep interconnection. It is something that we 'see', rather than something we formulate logically. For Lewis, the Christian faith offers us a means of seeing things properly – as they really are, despite their outward appearances. Christianity provides an intellectually capacious and imaginatively satisfying way of seeing things and grasping their interconnectedness, even if we find it difficult to express this in words.

Lewis's strong belief in the reasonableness of the Christian faith rests on his own quite distinct way of *seeing* the rationality of the created order and its ultimate grounding in God. Let's go back to Lewis's line about the sun letting us see things. Using this powerful image, Lewis invites us to see God as both the ground of the rationality of the world and the one who enables us to grasp that rationality. Lewis helps us to appreciate that Christianity gives us a standpoint from which we may survey things and grasp their intrinsic coherence. We *see* how things connect together.

This basic idea is found in one of the great works of medieval literature, which Lewis loved – Dante's *Divine Comedy*, written in the fourteenth century. The great Florentine poet and theologian here expresses the idea that Christianity provides a vision of things – something wonderful that can be *seen*, but is very difficult to express in words:

> From that moment onwards my power of sight exceeded
> That of speech, which fails at such a vision.[15]

G.K. Chesterton made the point that a reliable theory allows us to see things properly: 'We put on the theory, like a magic hat, and history becomes translucent like a house of glass.'[16] For Chesterton, a good theory is to be judged by the amount of illumination it offers and its capacity to accommodate what we see in the world around us and experience within us. 'With this idea once inside our heads, a million things become transparent as if a lamp were lit behind them.'[17] In the same way, Chesterton argued, Christianity validates itself by its ability to make sense of our observations of the world. 'The phenomenon does not prove Religion, but religion explains the Phenomenon.'[18]

Lewis consistently uses a remarkably wide range of visual metaphors – such as sun, light, blindness and shadows – to help us grasp the nature of a true understanding of things. This has two important results. First, it means that Lewis sees reason and imagination as working *together*, not *against each other*. Second, it leads Lewis to make extensive use of analogies in his apologetics, to enable us to *see* things in a new way. For example, Lewis's famous defence of the doctrine of the Trinity in *Mere Christianity* suggests that our difficulties with this notion arise mainly because we don't see it properly. If we see it another way – as, for example, an inhabitant of a two-dimensional world might try to grasp and describe the structure of a three-dimensional reality – then we begin to grasp why it makes so much sense: 'Try seeing it this way!'

Lewis does not try to prove the existence of God on purely rational grounds. His approach is much more interesting. Instead of launching an argument for the existence of God, Lewis invites us to see how what we observe in the world around us and experience within us fits into the Christian way of seeing things. Lewis's genius as an apologist – which we shall explore in more detail later – lay in his ability to show how a Christian viewpoint was able to offer a more satisfactory explanation of common human experience than its rivals, especially the atheism he had once himself so enthusiastically advocated.

Throughout his apologetic writings Lewis appeals to shared human experience and observation. How do we make sense of what we experience within us or observe outside us? Lewis came to realise that the Christian way of looking at things seemed to fit things in much better than the alternatives.

Fitting Things In: The Case of Longing

Let's look at an example – Lewis's 'argument from desire'. This is not really an argument at all. It is more about noticing how theory and observation fit together. It is a bit like trying on a hat or shirt for size and looking at yourself in a mirror. How well does it fit? How many of our observations of the world can a theory accommodate, and how persuasively does it do this? Lewis's 'argument from desire' invites us to notice how easily and naturally our experiences of desire fit into a Christian framework.

As we saw earlier, Lewis argues that we have desires and longings that no experience in this world seems able to satisfy. So how do we explain these? Lewis offers three explanations. First, we are never satisfied because we are looking for the wrong thing in this world. We must extend the scope of our search! Then we will eventually stumble across what will really make us happy. This, Lewis suggests, just leads to a long and hopeless search for something we never find. Or, second, we might give up in despair, believing there is nothing that will ever satisfy us. Why bother looking? Let's just give up.

But Lewis believes there is a third answer – one that chimes in with his own experience. When we see these longings through the lens of the Christian faith, we realise that they are exactly what we would expect if Christianity is true. Christianity tells us that this is not our true home and that we were created for heaven. 'If I find in myself a desire which no experience in this world can satisfy, the most probable explanation is that I was made for another world.'[19]

Lewis's *explicit* appeal to reason thus involves an *implicit* appeal to the imagination. Perhaps this helps us understand why Lewis appeals to both modern and postmodern readers. Lewis gives us a way of looking at things that bridges the great divide between modernity and postmodernity. Each outlook has its strengths because it is part of a greater whole. Their weaknesses arise when they pretend to offer the full picture, when they really offer only part of the whole. Once the full 'big picture' is seen, they are both seen in their proper light.

One of the reasons Lewis embraced Christianity is that it helped him to discern meaning in life. Life is about more than just understanding things: it is about being able to cope with ambiguity and bewilderment, and about finding something worthwhile to give us direction and meaning.

The Panorama and the Snapshots

So how did Christianity help Lewis find meaning? One way was for him to realise that there is a 'big picture' which makes sense of 'little pictures'. Or, to change the image slightly, there is a panorama into which each of the snapshots fits. Lewis doesn't use this way of speaking, but it is a good way of representing his basic approach. Lewis explained the importance of such a 'big picture' in 1936, when reflecting on medieval literature – such as Dante's famous *Divine Comedy*, which offered a persuasive imaginative vision of a unified cosmic and world order. Lewis remarked that works such as the *Divine Comedy* reflected a 'unity of the highest order' because they are able to cope with 'the greatest diversity of subordinated detail'.[20] Lewis's language here is technical and precise. There is a certain way of seeing things that brings them into the sharpest focus, illuminating the shadows and allowing an underlying unity to be seen. This, for Lewis, is a 'realising imagination' – a way of seeing or 'picturing' reality that is faithful to the way things actually are.[21]

We need to unpack this idea a little more to appreciate the point that Lewis is making. His basic idea is that Christianity sets out a way of seeing things which does two important things. First, it declares that the world is not meaningless, chaotic, or pointless. The world may look fuzzy and out of focus, so that we can't see a pattern. But that's because we need a lens to bring it into focus. For Lewis, Christianity provides a lens that allows us to see things more clearly. Or, to switch images, instead of just hearing a noise, we hear a melody.

Second, Lewis tells us that this 'big picture' helps make sense of its individual details – such as our own lives. We fit into something bigger. We're in the picture, and are meant to be there. The picture is not complete without us. We realise that our familiar world is to be understood as a reflection of something more lasting and solid. Grasping this greater view of things helps us understand our own world – and ourselves – better.

Lewis was in good company here. The novelist Dorothy L. Sayers also discovered the remarkable ability of the Christian faith to make sense of things, and she saw this as a clear indication of its truth. Christian belief, she wrote to a colleague, 'seems to offer the only explanation of the universe that is intellectually satisfactory'.[22] Indeed, Sayers was so attracted to this aspect of Christianity that at times she wondered whether she had 'fallen in love with an intellectual pattern'.[23] Lewis, in contrast, saw Christianity's ability to make sense of things as part of its attraction. But there were other benefits as well – not least the immense stimulus it provided for his imaginative life and his exploration of the theme of beauty.

So what difference does this make? Perhaps the easiest way of explaining this is to compare Richard Dawkins and C.S. Lewis. For Dawkins, there is no meaning or purpose in the universe. Nor is there any notion of goodness. That doesn't stop us from inventing ideas of meaning or goodness. But we're basing our lives on something make-believe. We're pretending that there is meaning to our lives, or that there are certain moral values that are reliable. But deep down, we know they're just our inventions, things we have created to help us cope with life and struggle with its puzzles and pain.

Lewis offers us a very different approach. There is meaning to life. There is a deeper moral order within the universe. And once we discover these, we can base our lives on them. This is not about *inventing* goodness and meaning but about *discerning* them. Lewis discovered that God was the one who both *disclosed* and *safeguarded* meaning and morality. We are invited to enter into a new way of seeing things, which is also the *right* way of seeing things – not because anyone imposes it on us, but because we have discovered it and realised its reliability and trustworthiness.

Basing our lives on this meaning changes our perspective. As G.K. Chesterton points out, knowing that there is a deeper meaning makes life more interesting: 'One can find no meanings in a jungle of scepticism; but the man will find more and more meanings who walks through a forest of doctrine and design. Here everything has a story tied to its tail.'[24]

But more than making life more interesting, discerning meaning invests our lives with significance. No longer are we mere observers. Instead, we have a role to play and an obligation to play it. At the end of Lewis's sermon 'The Weight of Glory', he addresses the burden that this meaning places on us. Our future glory (and that of our neighbours) should change the way we live our lives now:

The load, or weight, or burden of my neighbour's glory should be laid daily on my back . . . There are no ordinary people. You have never talked to a mere mortal. Nations, cultures, arts, civilisation – these are mortal, and their life is to ours as the life of a gnat. But it is immortals whom we joke with, work with, marry, snub, and exploit – immortal horrors or everlasting splendours . . . Our charity must be a real and costly love, with deep feeling for the sins in spite of which we love the sinner . . . Next to the Blessed Sacrament itself, your neighbour is the holiest object presented to your senses.[25]

This perspective is very different from the self-centred, 'let us eat and drink for tomorrow we die' attitude that is so prevalent in the world. And this perspective is also part of the reason why so many social services, charities and hospitals find their roots in Christianity. Meaning matters. When we form a proper response to the question of what life is all about, it brings our lives into focus and in turn points our gaze outwards.

Now there's a lot more to say about this, and we'll come back to some of these points later in our reflections. But that's enough for our first conversation! Let's take a break, and prepare to join Lewis again for our next meeting, when we will think about the importance of friendship.

2

'Old Friends to Trust':
C.S. Lewis on Friendship

Friendship is unnecessary, like philosophy, like art, like the universe itself (for God did not need to create). It has no survival value; rather it is one of those things which give value to survival.

C.S. Lewis, 'Equality'

At our second meeting with Lewis, we might ask him to tell us about the Inklings. Who were they? How did they operate? How much does Lewis's own work owe to the group? After all, everyone who is familiar with C.S. Lewis wants to know more about the Inklings – the astonishingly creative group of writers and thinkers who met at Oxford in the 1930s and 1940s and helped shape some of the classics of twentieth-century literature.

Lewis, however, might suggest that we talk about something more fundamental – friendship. Lewis was no solitary genius who lived and worked in isolation. He needed friends to support and encourage him. He needed friends who could inspire him – to enable him to become a better person and a better writer. Some of Lewis's friends, such as Arthur Greeves, gave him emotional support; others, such as J.R.R. Tolkien, gave him intellectual encouragement. And Lewis's conversion – first to belief in God, and then to Christianity – owed an incalculable amount to his close friends such as Owen Barfield and Tolkien.

That's why Lewis would want us to talk about friendship first. Without his friends, Lewis would never have become a spiritual and literary giant. And he would have little hesitation in demanding that we treat the questions of friendship with the greatest seriousness: What kind of friends do we have? How much time do we spend nurturing our friendships? What's the nature of real friendship? These aren't secondary questions as we might assume, but essential ones for living life well. Friends matter. They matter at school. They matter at work. They matter even more in old age. That's why so many nod their heads at a neat epigram from Francis Bacon: 'Old wood best to burn, old wine to drink, old friends to trust, and old authors to read.'

We all need friends – people who care for us, who can share our moments of joy, and who will support us in times of need and difficulty. Old friends tend to be good and true friends. Friends encourage us when we are downhearted and demoralised, they motivate us to perform better, and they help us pick up the pieces when things go wrong.

We know that friends are important, but we live in a world that often trivialises the nature of friendship. Online social networks, with their collections of 'friends', have in many people's lives overtaken the place of real friendship. Yet despite these networks touting increased connectivity, research has shown that the upshot is less satisfaction with life.[1] These 'friendships' are leaving us worse off than before.

So what might Lewis have to say to us about real friendship? Why is it important? What are its purposes and its pleasures? What are its benefits – and its risks? And how should friendships function?

As a student of the classics at Oxford University in the early 1920s, Lewis would have been aware of the rich classical notion of friendship. Classical civilisation regarded friendship as one of the greatest privileges and responsibilities. Aristotle drew a distinction between genuine friendships and relationships that were based simply on need and pleasure. Such need- or pleasure-based friendships lasted only as long as they were useful or enjoyable – what we might call 'fair-weather friends'. But real friendship, Aristotle argued, went much deeper. Friends care for each other. Aristotle suggested that someone would wish the best for his or her friend, not because it might be of personal benefit, but because it enriched the friend.

For Aristotle, friendship is about bringing out what is best in people. The best friends share a common vision of what is good and important, and help each other achieve goodness. Friends 'enlarge and extend each other's moral experience' by providing 'a mirror in which the other may see himself'.[2] This kind of friendship rests on shared assumptions about the nature of goodness and what might be involved in living the good life. It is not a casual matter, but something deep, enabling each other to become – and remain – good people.

But Lewis did more than just study what others had to say about friendship. He wrote about it at length in a book of his own, *The Four Loves*.

The Four Loves

The success of Lewis's Broadcast Talks for the BBC during the Second World War (the basis for his book *Mere Christianity*) led to lots more invitations to record radio addresses. He ignored these requests – except for one. In August 1958, Lewis recorded four hour-long talks on love for the Episcopal Radio-TV Foundation in Atlanta, Georgia. Each of the talks was devoted to one of four 'loves' – affection, friendship, eros (sexual love) and charity. Lewis's book *The Four Loves* (1960) was based on these talks. It remains a provocative and helpful exploration of aspects of love – including friendship. The book distils Lewis's accumulated wisdom over the years, perhaps most effectively in his discussion of the value and role of friends.

This late work is unusual in some respects. For a start, Lewis's trademark use of stories and anecdotes is largely absent from this work. The few that he does use – such as Mrs Fidget – are memorable precisely because they stand out in a text from which they are otherwise conspicuously absent. Second, love is analysed in a curiously detached, almost clinical manner. Yet by the time of writing this work, completed in June 1959, Lewis had married Joy Davidman. If Lewis experienced love as a searing and overwhelming human emotion, there is little sign of it in *The Four Loves*. The reader who was unaware that Lewis had recently married would not have guessed it from the disengaged account presented in the book. In marked contrast, *A Grief Observed* (1961) represents one of the finest accounts of the emotional firestorm unleashed by bereavement. Lewis could write with emotional power and depth when he wanted to, yet he did not choose to do so here.

So what does Lewis think is so important about friendship? Lewis sees friendship as something vital and transformative. Yet friendship is a means to an end, not an end in itself. Only very inadequate or ambitious people deliberately set out to secure friends as a means of boosting their own self-confidence or advancing their own ends. The wise set out to achieve something more important and noble, and find that their friends enable them to do this. 'The very condition of having Friends is that we should want something else besides Friends.'[3] As Lewis rightly observes, this means that friendship is not about moral improvement. It 'makes good men better and bad men worse'. Yet where there is good, friendship enables it to be achieved and maintained.

Lewis makes it clear that a 'friend' is more than just an acquaintance. 'Many people when they speak of their "friends" mean only their companions.'[4] Following Aristotle, Lewis insisted that friendship arose when two people realised that they 'have in common some insight or interest or even taste which the others do not share and which, till that moment, each believed to be his own unique treasure (or burden)'.[5] For Lewis, friendship extends to the exploration of the deepest questions of life.

> *Do you love me?* means *Do you see the same truth?* – or at least, 'Do you *care about* the same truth?' The man who agrees with us that some question, little regarded by others, is of great importance, can be our friend. He need not agree with us about the answer.

Lewis's analysis helps us make sense of how his friends helped him to write books and cope with life's disappointments and challenges.

Lewis's early letters and diaries suggest that he had a very small social circle, being seen as difficult or awkward by his fellow students. We don't know why they called him 'Heavy Lewis' as an undergraduate. The most likely explanation is that he was seen as 'heavy going', out of touch with mainstream student life at the time, especially by the 'hearties', who excelled at sport and heavy drinking. Perhaps Lewis's friends came to matter to him because they were so few in number.

When I was researching my recent biography of Lewis, I began to appreciate how important friends became to him. Lewis formed very strong attachments to a relatively small number of people. Without those friends, Lewis would have been a lesser person. Time and time again, Lewis's friends provided him with support in seasons of difficulty and with inspiration for his books and writing.

Yet Lewis's friendships were not always easy. Sometimes they went wrong – as in the case of the increasingly distant relationship between Lewis and Tolkien. They also went wrong at Magdalen College, Oxford, where by 1949 factions had developed within its governing body, several of which were hostile to Lewis. This increasingly uncomfortable atmosphere at Magdalen College was a significant contributing factor to Lewis's decision to move to Cambridge several years later.

So imagine that we are having lunch with Lewis. The topic of friendship is on the agenda. Perhaps the most obvious starting point is to ask Lewis to tell us about some of the important people in his life and the difference that they made to him.

Lewis's Core Friendships

Lewis's first real friendship was with his elder brother, Warren ('Warnie'). After the family moved to their new home ('Little Lea'), Warnie and Lewis became close friends. At that time, the threat of disease led many middle-class families in their part of Belfast to keep children indoors. The children had little option other than to read books or play games together. Lewis and Warnie read widely and created imaginary literary worlds. Later, the two brothers brought their stories about 'Animal-Land' and 'India' together in a composite world, 'Boxen'.

In the summer of 1907, Flora Lewis took her two sons to France. In those days, few Irish people travelled abroad. While their father stayed at home to work in his law office in Belfast, the rest of the Lewis family travelled to France and stayed in a small family hotel on the Normandy coastline. Yet only a year later, Flora Lewis died, slowly and painfully, of cancer in the autumn of 1908, before Lewis's tenth birthday. His world fell to pieces around him. Warnie was Lewis's only companion for the next few years, while they studied at boarding schools in England, far away from their family in Ireland.

A new friendship began to emerge in April 1914, when Lewis was home during school vacation. Arthur Greeves, the son of a prosperous Belfast linen manufacturer, lived close to Little Lea. Greeves was in poor health and was confined to bed for much of the time. To Lewis's surprise, he was invited to visit Greeves. Lewis went somewhat reluctantly.

Around that time, Lewis had developed a love for Norse mythology. On being shown into Greeves's bedroom, Lewis noticed that Greeves had been reading a book on that subject. He suddenly became interested. 'Do *you* like that?' he asked, pointing at the book. Greeves was delighted.[6] Their shared interest in what Lewis called 'Northernness' became the initial basis of their long-standing friendship, which lasted until Lewis's death in 1963. They exchanged letters regularly. Especially in the 1910s and 1920s, Greeves became Lewis's confidant – someone he could talk to about the things that really mattered to him or were troubling him.

Yet there were serious differences between the two. For a start, Lewis was a somewhat aggressive atheist, and Greeves was a committed Christian. It soon became clear that their disagreement on this matter was so serious that they gave up talking about it. When Lewis moved to Oxford in 1917, he developed a mild interest in sadomasochism, which clearly shocked Greeves. Yet Lewis needed someone who would listen to him on these matters – who would stay friends with him, even though he disagreed with Lewis's new interests. In the end, this turned out to be a phase that Lewis needed to work through. Further tensions arose in the relationship in the late 1910s when Greeves told Lewis that he was beginning to realise he was a homosexual. Lewis made it clear that he did not see this as interfering with their relationship, which continued unaffected.

Greeves became a sounding board for Lewis – someone whose judgement he trusted and whose advice he sought. In 1917, Greeves was the only person Lewis told about his increasingly complicated relationship with Mrs Moore, the mother of his close friend Paddy, who had been killed in the First World War. When Lewis began to embrace Christianity in 1931, he wrote two letters to Greeves telling him about both this development and the reasons underlying it. The second letter, written weeks after the event, sets out Lewis's thinking in considerable detail and is of critical importance in understanding Lewis's decisive move from believing in God to believing in Christianity.

Yet Greeves was no academic, and could not cope with the questions Lewis was beginning to explore about the purpose and place of literature and how Christianity was to be expressed and explored. As their correspondence makes clear, Lewis found Greeves invaluable in helping him think about more personal matters. Yet Lewis also needed friends who shared his academic interests and could help him reflect on the deeper questions raised by his studies.

As might be expected, Lewis formed new friendships with other students during his time as an undergraduate at Oxford University. The most important of Lewis's student friends was Owen Barfield, an undergraduate at Wadham College, Oxford, whom Lewis met in 1919. Barfield was unquestionably Lewis's intellectual equal, and possibly his superior. In 1920, Barfield was awarded first-class honours in English Language and Literature.

Their disagreement in the initial phase of their lifelong friendship was so severe that Lewis came to refer to this as their 'Great War'. Yet Lewis relished this engagement, seeing Barfield as 'the best and wisest of my unofficial teachers' at Oxford. Barfield played a decisive role in undermining Lewis's atheism, emphasising the incoherence of reductionist ways of thinking. Lewis trusted him, and respected his intellectual judgement. When Barfield raised questions about Lewis's atheism, Lewis knew that he had no other choice than to take them seriously. Barfield's persistent questioning eventually forced Lewis to the conclusion that his atheism was incoherent.

After leaving Oxford, Barfield went on to establish a successful legal practice in London from 1934 to 1959. His clients, needless to say, included Lewis, who asked his old friend to administer his estate after his death. Lewis knew whom he could trust.

Lewis's Friendship with J.R.R. Tolkien

When Lewis became an Oxford don in 1925, his circle of friends began to expand beyond his childhood and student friends. The most important of Lewis's new friends was J.R.R. Tolkien, a philologist who was Oxford University's Professor of Anglo-Saxon. Like Lewis, Tolkien had been an officer in the British army during the First World War and had returned to the academic life after his demobilisation. Tolkien was fascinated by the languages and lore of Northern Europe and founded a study group he named the 'Kolbítar', aimed at fostering an appreciation of Old Norse and its associated literature. (Tolkien borrowed this name from an Icelandic word meaning 'coal-biters', which was a derisive term for Norsemen who refused to join in the hunt or fight battles.) Lewis found this 'little Icelandic club' a massive stimulus to his imagination, throwing him back into 'a wild dream of northern skies and Valkyrie music'.[7]

The friendship between Tolkien and Lewis proved to be of critical importance for twentieth-century English literature. It is no exaggeration to say that this friendship gave birth to both Tolkien's *Lord of the Rings* and Lewis's Chronicles of Narnia. It all began when Tolkien asked Lewis if he would look over a piece of writing that he had just completed, and let him know what he thought of it. What Tolkien wanted Lewis to read was a long narrative poem titled *The Lay of Leithian*. It was a precursor to the great work that we now know as *The Lord of the Rings*.

It is clear Tolkien needed a 'critical friend' at this point, a mentor who would encourage and criticise, affirm and improve his writing. Tolkien had had such 'critical friends' in the past. Yet these friendships had faded and Tolkien needed someone he could trust to help him move ahead with his writing. And what Tolkien needed he found in Lewis.

The two men encouraged each other to write. Since they each had a high estimation of the other's judgements, they read their writings to each other. In the early 1930s, Tolkien read parts of *The Hobbit* to Lewis; Lewis read parts of *The Pilgrim's Regress* to Tolkien.

While Lewis helped Tolkien in many ways, his most important achievement lay in persuading Tolkien to finish what he was writing. Tolkien was a perfectionist, always wanting to revise documents again and again, and somehow never finishing them. Lewis gave Tolkien the encouragement he needed to complete his masterpiece. As Tolkien later recalled, Lewis was for many years the only audience for *The Lord of the Rings*. 'But for his interest and unceasing eagerness for more I should never have brought *The L. of the R.* to a conclusion.'[8]

Tolkien's influence on Lewis's Chronicles of Narnia was more indirect. In September 1931, Lewis invited Tolkien and another friend to join him for dinner at Magdalen College. In the course of a long walk through the college's gardens afterwards, Tolkien helped Lewis appreciate the deep appeal of Christianity. As a result of talking to Tolkien, Lewis realised that Christianity was a 'true myth' – that is to say, a true way of expressing reality in narrative form. The Chronicles of Narnia arose some twenty years later from this basic insight, and are now widely regarded as one of the finest retellings of the Christian story.

But Tolkien did not like the Chronicles of Narnia. He regarded them as being hastily written. They mingled different kinds of myths. (What was Father Christmas doing in Narnia?) Most worrying for Tolkien, Lewis seemed to have 'borrowed' ideas from his own early drafts of *The Lord of the Rings*. By the time the final book in the Chronicles of Narnia was published in 1956, Lewis's relationship with Tolkien was in trouble.

What had gone wrong? Lewis's friendship with Tolkien was at its strongest throughout the 1930s – an immensely creative period for both men. Yet it began to falter in the early 1940s as Lewis developed a friendship with the novelist Charles Williams, who had recently settled in Oxford. Tolkien felt he had been displaced in Lewis's affections and resented Lewis's growing intimacy with Williams. Tolkien's suspicions in the early 1950s that Lewis had plagiarised material from *The Lord of the Rings* made things worse. Finally, Lewis's clandestine civil marriage to Joy Davidman caused Tolkien considerable distress, partly because he did not approve of civil marriages, but mainly because Lewis never told him about it. It became clear to him that Lewis no longer regarded him as a close friend.

During this period of increasing alienation, however, both men retained their respect and admiration for each other. Tolkien was instrumental in persuading Lewis to accept the newly established Chair of Medieval and Renaissance English at Cambridge University in 1954. And recently discovered documents show that Lewis proposed Tolkien for the 1961 Nobel Prize in Literature, citing *The Lord of the Rings* as a justification for this honour.

It is clear that the rupture in Lewis's and Tolkien's friendship was due primarily to Tolkien. To an outsider, Tolkien may seem to have been somewhat oversensitive, overreacting to developments which were not malicious or sinister. Yet perhaps this reminds us that friendships cannot be taken for granted. They require investment and maintenance if they are to flourish.

The Inklings

What is probably the most important friendship of Lewis's life was communal rather than individual – the remarkable group we remember today as the Inklings.

Lewis's social life entered a new phase in 1930. His brother, Warnie, who had been on active military service, announced his decision to retire from the British army. At that time, Warnie had been posted to Shanghai in China – one of many overseas postings which prevented the two brothers from spending time together. At Lewis's suggestion, Warnie moved to Oxford and moved in with Lewis and Mrs Moore and her daughter, Maureen. A new house was purchased – The Kilns – which could be extended to give everyone enough living room. Lewis was delighted. He and Warnie would be together again. Their friendship could resume after a long interruption.

Once Warnie had settled into Oxford, he became involved in Lewis's literary life. He worked in Lewis's rooms in Magdalen College, typing up the Lewis family history. Warnie had a love of French history and began to research some projects that eventually led to a well-received series of books, such as *The Splendid Century: Some Aspects of French Life in the Reign of Louis XIV* (1953). Lewis and Tolkien were already meeting regularly in Lewis's rooms by this stage to discuss their various projects. It seemed entirely natural that Warnie should join them. And gradually, still others – such as Owen Barfield, Hugo Dyson and Nevill Coghill – joined as well. As Tolkien later remarked, it was an 'undetermined and unelected circle of friends'.[9] They had two shared interests: Christianity and literature. Lewis referred to the group as the Inklings, and that name has stuck.

The group – all of whom were men – got into the habit of meeting twice a week. On Tuesday mornings, they gathered in The Eagle and Child public house in Oxford's St Giles – a broad, tree-lined street, heading north from the centre of town – to exchange news and gossip. The second meeting was business rather than social. On Thursday evenings, they met in Lewis's rooms in Magdalen College to discuss works in preparation – mainly by Lewis himself, Tolkien and Charles Williams – such as early drafts of Tolkien's *The Lord of the Rings*.

It is important not to overstate the importance of the group. Charles Williams, for example, had already written some of his finest works before moving to Oxford and joining the Inklings. Tolkien was both stubbornly independent and sensitive, and found it difficult to accept criticism. Lewis never submitted the text of any of his Narnia novels to the group. Yet each of these authors submitted work for discussion, and each was of the view that these works benefited considerably from discussion. Among the works discussed by the Inklings, we may note Lewis's *Out of the Silent Planet* and *Perelandra*, and Charles Williams's *All Hallows Eve*.

The Inklings are now widely acclaimed as one of the greatest literary clubs of the twentieth century. Without naming either the group or its members in *The Four Loves*, Lewis reflected on the importance of a 'circle of friends' such as the Inklings as the nucleus of a 'rebellion of serious thinkers against accepted clap-trap'.[10] To challenge the status quo demands fellowship and commitment. Furthermore, Lewis emphasised the privilege of being part of such a group. 'In a good Friendship, every member often feels humility towards the rest. He sees that they are splendid, and counts himself lucky to be among them.'[11]

So why did the group work so well? And what can we learn from its success? Let's tease out the elements that made the Inklings so successful.

First, they were primarily a group of *friends*. They knew and respected one another. In one sense, the Inklings can be seen as a gathering of friends of Lewis (especially) and Tolkien. Yet this misses the point that the Inklings generated a network of friendships. Members knew they were respected and could say what they really thought. Newcomers were carefully vetted and outsiders were discouraged from attending. At times, Lewis would have to restore order when things got out of hand. Hugo Dyson, for example, found Tolkien's stories of orcs and elves tedious and wanted everyone to know that. Yet overall, the group worked well.

Second, the Inklings were a *community* – a group of like-minded people with similar interests and concerns, and above all a love of literature. In a sense, they were amateurs – people who loved literature for its own sake rather than for professional advancement, and who saw the promotion of good literature as a worthy end in itself. John Wain, one of the members of the group, later emphasised how the Inklings saw themselves as a countercultural community, trying to reclaim a noble approach to literature which had fallen out of fashion, by 'redirecting the whole current of contemporary art and life'.[12]

Yet perhaps it is the third aspect of the Inklings that helps us grasp the reason for their success. They were *critical* friends – that is to say, they trusted one another and their judgements, and had earned the right to comment on one another's works. At times, there were tensions between those who wrote and those who merely commented. Yet the underlying intention was clear. Criticism was about offering external perspectives, allowing an author to appreciate how his readers might understand him, rather than how he understood himself. Criticism was not seen as a cheap way of scoring points, of boosting one's own self-esteem, or of making fun of a colleague. At its heart, the enterprise of criticism was about taking something that was good and making it even better.

This is an important point. In everyday use, *criticism* means saying negative things about something. As the Inklings understood it, however, the word meant judging something, identifying both its strengths and weaknesses. In everyday use, the word is purely negative; as Lewis and his colleagues understood it, the word mingled positive and negative elements, reflecting that any work under discussion would have qualities that needed to be affirmed and flaws that needed further attention. Some, such as Tolkien, found criticism difficult to accept. Yet what we know of these meetings indicates that the group saw itself as a catalyst for improvement – and for offering encouragement.

That brings us neatly to the final point. The Inklings offered a supportive and encouraging environment, which helped its members strengthen and complete their works. This was especially important for Tolkien, who was clearly discouraged by anxieties about how his work would be received by his critics and kept revising texts to the point that many believed they would never be published. The diaries and letters of individual Inklings help us appreciate the level of support they gave to each other at their Thursday gatherings.

So what can we learn from these reflections on the Inklings? One of the most obvious points is the importance of support and encouragement in doing something that matters. For Lewis and Tolkien, writing was of central importance to their lives. Lewis always found that others could help him write – by encouraging him to write, by assessing what he had written, and by helping him to sort out the structure of works he hoped to write. Although Lewis was the author of all his works, most of them were seasoned and finely honed through interaction with other people whose views he trusted.

The success of the Inklings also helps us to see criticism in a positive light. There are, unfortunately, people who boost their own sense of importance by criticising others as a matter of principle. Yet within this community, criticism was a mark of respect and commitment. It marked commitment on the part of the Inklings both to the member whose work was being discussed and to the work under consideration. The objective was simple: to take a promising text and make it still better. In a paradoxical sense, criticism offered was thus seen as an affirmation that this text was worth attention.

Lewis's analysis of the 'circle of friends' at times echoes the imagery of a church or religious community, bonded together by a shared commitment to truth and to communicating and commending this effectively. Lewis makes clear the limits of an individual; the 'circle of friends' compensates for an individual's weaknesses and enhances his or her strengths. These comments are particularly important in light of Lewis's frequent admission that he found himself wearied by his apologetic ministry, which left him feeling emptied and isolated – a matter to which we shall return in a later conversation. The 'circle of friends' was an important antidote to this sense of isolation and loneliness.

Yet in contrast to this 'circle of friends' image, Lewis also warns us that friendship can go badly wrong. It's not just that relationships break down. It's that we can idolise friendship, or abuse it. In 1944, Lewis gave a lecture at King's College London on 'The Inner Ring'.[13] What did Lewis mean by this phrase 'Inner Ring'? Basically, he was talking about an 'in group', a select few self-important individuals who saw themselves as defining what was good and right. For people within the 'Inner Ring', saying that 'He's not one of us' means 'He doesn't belong' or 'He's not the right kind of person'.

Friendship in the 'Inner Ring' is used as a means of gaining admittance to the circles of power. Friendship itself is not what really matters – it is an instrument which opens doors and secures influence. It makes us feel that we matter and are important. Lewis illustrates this from a commonplace at Oxford University – being asked to be an examiner (one of Oxford's dullest academic responsibilities):

> It is a terrible bore, of course, when old Fatty Smithson draws you aside and whispers, 'Look here, we've got to get you in on this examination somehow' or 'Charles and I saw at once that you've got to be on this committee.' A terrible bore . . . ah, but how much more terrible if you were left out! It is tiring and unhealthy to lose your Saturday afternoons: but to have them free because you don't matter, that is much worse.[14]

Lewis rightly points out that this desire to be part of the 'Inner Ring' is not really about friendship at all. It is about our own insecurity and yearning to matter. It is about using 'friends' as tools to gain what we want. We value someone, not because of who they are, but because of what they can do for us. We want them to boost our self-esteem and self-importance and get us privileged access to things we might otherwise not be able to get at all. In fact, our longing to be part of an 'Inner Ring' debases friendship. *Real* friendship is about shared affection, respect and interests. As Lewis concluded, there is 'no "inside" that is worth reaching'. What really matters is friendship, pure and simple.

So what might we conclude? Perhaps the most important point to take away from our time with Lewis is that friendship is of vital importance because friendship is transformational – both for ourselves and for our friends. This is key because any form of ministry or service or endeavour worth pursuing requires support and fellowship. It cannot be undertaken in isolation. Friendship is essential to fit us for the task. That's why the questions of friendship should be ones we ask ourselves on a regular basis: How are my friends influencing me? What task lies ahead of me that demands a community of support? How can I support my friends? Am I spending enough time and energy cultivating real friendships? And is friendship an end or a means – something good in itself or a good to be consumed? It is no wonder that so many successful churches encourage small groups to meet and discuss things that concern them. Lewis himself gave and received this kind of support. We must expect to do the same.

We've now had two meetings with Lewis, and we haven't thoroughly explored his most famous creation – Narnia. It's time to change that. Let's imagine that we're meeting Lewis at one of his favourite haunts, and that Narnia is on our agenda. In our next two encounters with Lewis, we'll explore how he used the story of Narnia to open up a deeper vision of reality.

3

A Story-Shaped World: C.S. Lewis on Narnia and the Importance of Stories

'Child,' said the Voice [of Aslan], 'I am telling you your story, not hers. I tell no one any story but his own.'

C.S. Lewis, *The Horse and His Boy*

It's time for our meeting with Lewis, and it's bound to be a lively discussion. We are going to talk about the Chronicles of Narnia, after all; the series that many consider C.S. Lewis's masterpiece. Yet before we can get to the questions we've prepared – How was it written? What was its inspiration? – Lewis, unsurprisingly, has a question for us.

Which story are you in?

To our more modern ears, this seems an odd way to begin a chat about Narnia, a story for children, but Lewis is concerned with something deeper, something more fundamental than how his series came into being. He is addressing the questions at the core of our lives.

Each of us naturally lives within a story, a 'meta-narrative' that shapes our lives, whether we are aware of this fact or not. Some of us live under the assumptions of the Western story of societal progress, that civilisation – technologically, socially, or morally – is continually improving. Others live under the story of individual progress of the sort peddled on daytime talk shows, that the self is the most important thing there is and that more or better information will organically produce better selves. Still others subscribe to the victim meta-narrative, that their personal choices have little impact on the world they live in.

So again, Lewis asks us, *Which story are you in? Have you chosen your story wisely? Have you challenged the story you tell yourself, if it doesn't align with reality?* These questions might not be the ones that come first to our minds, especially in a discussion of Narnia. But what Lewis is saying is that the questions that *appear* more pressing in our lives, such as 'How do I make myself more successful?' are built on shaky assumptions from a story that may be distorting reality.

Looking back on his time as an atheist, Lewis was appalled at how easily he had been unthinkingly captivated by the metanarrative of his day. How, he wondered, could he have been so blind? Why was he taken in by it? 'I must have been as blind as a bat not to have seen, long before, the ludicrous contradiction between my theory of life and my actual experiences.'[1] In the end, the power of this captivating metanarrative was broken only when he realised that there was a more powerful, more appealing and more realistic metanarrative – the compelling Christian 'big story' of creation and redemption.

What is the best story about the world? What is the most satisfying and realistic metanarrative? These may not seem like pressing questions, but Lewis would demand that we take them with the greatest seriousness. As we saw in chapter 1, which story we believe we are in has a huge impact on the way that we live.

It is so easy to be taken in – to be held captive, to be locked into a way of thinking which prevents us from seeing things as they really are and from becoming the people we are meant to be. We've got to get this right!

In his 1941 sermon 'The Weight of Glory', Lewis declares that our age is held captive. We are spellbound, caught up in a secular and secularising metanarrative that insists our destiny and good lie in this world. We are told – and come to believe – that the ideas of transcendent realms, of worlds to come, are simply illusions. Our educational system, Lewis notes with obvious sadness, has colluded with this modern myth – that the sources and goals of human good are 'found on this earth'.[2]

Lewis declares that the time has come to break free from this 'evil enchantment of worldliness'. Lewis has no doubt about what has to be done. So deeply has this 'evil enchantment' saturated our thinking that we need the 'strongest spell' to break its power. Lewis reminds his readers that 'spells are used for breaking enchantments as well as for inducing them'.[3] Christianity has to show that it can tell a more compelling and engaging story that will capture the imagination of its culture.

The imagined realm of Narnia is the spell that Lewis cast to help break the secular spell and open our imaginations and minds to another possibility.

The fabulous world of Narnia is now regarded as a classic in children's literature. Although Lewis had no children of his own, he somehow managed to connect with them in a way that few others could manage. Lewis remembered the deep delight he experienced during his own childhood when reading classic children's books of the Edwardian age. Yet the appeal of Lewis's genius for writing fiction was not limited to children. Many still find his science fiction trilogy deeply satisfying, just as some feel his late novel *Till We Have Faces* is the best thing he wrote.

But for most of Lewis's readers, his greatest achievement is the Chronicles of Narnia. The seven novels which make up the Chronicles of Narnia were published during the period of 1950 to 1956. The best known is the opening novel in the series, *The Lion, the Witch and the Wardrobe*, which introduces readers to the land of Narnia, the noble lion Aslan and the four Pevensie children – Peter, Susan, Edmund and Lucy.

Given the massive impact of Lewis's Chronicles of Narnia, it is important to appreciate that they were conceived when Lewis's personal life had hit an all-time low. In the late 1940s, Lewis's world was falling to pieces. England faced austerity measures – including food rationing – in the aftermath of the war. Lewis had been passed over for at least two major senior appointments at Oxford University. Tensions were building within the senior common room at Magdalen College. The Faculty of English was divided over its post-war direction. Lewis realised he was becoming dangerously isolated in his own college, among his faculty and in the university at large.

As if all this weren't enough, Lewis's personal life was a mess. Mrs Moore had developed dementia and was becoming difficult to manage. Lewis's brother, Warnie, who lived at The Kilns, was also becoming difficult – in his case because of alcoholism. Lewis was overworked, as the result of a rapid rise in student numbers at the end of the Second World War. His important wartime friendship with Charles Williams ended unexpectedly with Williams's death in 1945. And his friendship with Tolkien was beginning to break down.

Yet in the midst of this hopeless situation, the magical world of Narnia was born. Was writing Narnia a form of escapism? Was Lewis using his imagined world as a way of distracting himself from the bleak situation he now faced, professionally and personally? It's hard to rule out these possibilities. But it's much more likely that Lewis saw the writing of Narnia as a creative project that would be fun to develop, presenting him with a way to examine how a good story might explore theological ideas.

In our next two encounters with Lewis, we'll look at how the stories of Narnia open up some of the great questions of life. But today, we'll focus on why Lewis thought that stories were so important. After all, he wrote many works of fiction. So let's begin by talking about the importance of stories. Why write a story in the first place, instead of an essay on the meaning of life?

Breaking the Secular Spell: Lewis on Enchanting the Imagination

Lewis loved reading. Even in the early 1900s he found stories entrancing. His favourites included Beatrix Potter's *The Tale of Squirrel Nutkin* (1903), as well as some of Edith Nesbit's classic children's stories, including *Five Children and It* (1902), *The Phoenix and the Wishing Carpet* (1904) and *The Story of the Amulet* (1906). Later he encountered the 'fairy stories' of George MacDonald, which had a major impact on him. Although Lewis was quick to appreciate the imaginative appeal of stories, he seems to have been slower to realise how he could use them as ways of opening up deeper questions.

There seems to have been a number of aspects to Lewis's growing realisation that telling stories was an effective way of commending and communicating a worldview. The first was a turning point in Lewis's life – an extended conversation he had with his friends Hugo Dyson and J.R.R. Tolkien in September 1931. By that time, Lewis had begun to believe in God; he had not, however, made the transition to Christianity. Lewis's correspondence of the period makes it clear what his problem was. He did not see how the story of Jesus Christ could be of any relevance to us today.

Tolkien's reply to this question changed Lewis's outlook completely. Tolkien framed his reply using the word *myth* – a technical word which, unfortunately, is easily misunderstood. For most people, a 'myth' is a false story – maybe a story that was once thought to be true, or something that was invented to deceive people. Tolkien uses the term in a technical sense, to mean something like a 'grand narrative' or a 'narrated world-view'.[4] For Tolkien, the Gospels narrate 'a story of a larger kind' which embraces what is good, true and beautiful in the great myths of literature, expressing it as 'a far-off gleam or echo of *evangelium* in the real world'.[5]

What does Tolkien mean by this? Myths, he argues, are stories that people tell to make sense of the world. For Tolkien, Christianity brings to fulfilment the echoes and shadows of the truth that result from human questing and yearning. Human 'myths' allow a glimpse of a fragment of that truth, not its totality. They are like splintered fragments of the true light. Yet when the full and true story is told, it is able to bring to fulfilment all that was right and wise in those fragmentary visions of things.

For Tolkien, Christianity provides this total picture, which both unifies and transcends these fragmentary and imperfect insights. Christianity is a 'true myth'. It has the outward appearance of a 'myth' – a story about meaning. But this time, it really happened. And this story both makes sense of all the other stories that humans tell about themselves and their world, and provides their fulfilment.

Lewis found this insight to be life changing. First of all, it helped him to see how Christianity allowed him to view his beloved Norse myths in a new sense – not as something evil to be abandoned, but as an attempt to grasp something deeper, which ultimately proved to lie well beyond their reach. But more than this, it helped Lewis to realise the importance of stories.

A good story, Lewis realised, captivates the imagination. It can sneak past the 'watchful dragons' of a dogmatic rationalism. As Lewis himself discovered, fantasy works – such as the novels of George MacDonald – helped him realise the limits of his austere atheism. They showed him he was missing something in life, even though it would be some years before he worked out what it was. Could he help others do the same? After all, he was a professional teacher of literature. Why not write some literature, instead of just writing about it?

Lewis began to develop this idea seriously in the late 1930s. He had noted how H.G. Wells and others used works of science fiction to advance their secular humanism and optimism about the future of humanity. Lewis admired Wells as a storyteller, while at the same time cordially loathing the worldview so forcefully advocated in his stories.

Lewis wondered if he could use the same medium to challenge some of the naive assumptions of this outlook. The three works that resulted are usually referred to as the 'Space Trilogy' or the 'Ransom Trilogy' (after the chief character). In a letter from December 1938 to his friend Roger Lancelyn Green, Lewis remarked that he liked the 'whole interplanetary ideas as a *mythology*', and wanted to see whether he could use the genre to defend his own Christian point of view, rather than to surrender it to 'the opposite side'.[6]

So what did Lewis do? To put it simply, he wrote three works of science fiction which showed up secular evolutionary optimism as lightweight and naive, and highlighted the darker side of human nature.[7] The ideas that Lewis develops in these three novels are, of course, interesting. But what is even more interesting is the medium he uses to develop them – not a sustained logical argument which *tells* why secularist humanism has problems, but a winsome story which *shows* the same thing.[8]

How Lewis Came to Write Narnia

Lewis was regularly asked how he came to write the Chronicles of Narnia. He gave a number of answers. Let's try and weave them together.

Historically, the origins of Narnia seem to go back to the first phase of the Second World War. Britain declared war on Germany in September 1939. Widespread fear of destructive bombing raids on English cities led to children being evacuated to the relative safety of towns and cities in the countryside – such as Oxford. Mrs Moore welcomed four such 'evacuees' (as they were known) to The Kilns, who were duly followed by others. Lewis was astonished that the children had read so few books. They needed someone to read stories to them. Perhaps this gave Lewis the idea of writing some himself. Maureen Moore recalled Lewis's mentioning the idea of writing children's stories around this time.

Lewis realised that 'stories of this kind' could 'steal past a certain inhibition which had paralysed much of my own religion in childhood'.[9] What did Lewis mean by this? As a child, Lewis loved stories and had little interest in Christianity. But what if the medium he loved could have helped him embrace a faith that he clearly neither understood nor appreciated? What if stories could have opened up the wonder and joy of a faith that he had to wait two decades to discover? Lewis may well have written the books that he would have liked to read as a boy – as something that both excited his imagination and helped him to offer what he later called an 'imaginative welcome' to the Christian faith.

But Lewis also stressed the importance of images in the process of creating and writing Narnia. What sort of images? He mentions a few examples – such as a 'queen on a sledge' and a 'magnificent lion' – which became woven into his narrative. Some of these, he tells us, had been with him since he was about sixteen; it was, however, only when he was 'about 40' that he began to think about turning them into a story.[10]

At least to begin with, Lewis does not seem to have had a 'master plan' for the Chronicles of Narnia. *The Lion, the Witch and the Wardrobe* – the first and best in the series – can easily be read as a free-standing novel, complete in itself. Did Lewis originally intend to end things there? Perhaps. But the story told in this brilliant opening novel opens up further questions: Where did Narnia come from? How did it come to be in this mess? What happened next?

Lewis realised that he had told only part of the story of Narnia. He moved to develop his characters, allowing their own distinct personalities to emerge in the course of the story and according to its logic.

To appreciate Narnia to the full, it's important to respect it for what it is. J.R.R. Tolkien's *The Lord of the Rings* is a masterpiece of fine detail, with few loose ends left lying around. Narnia is rather different. Lewis wants to tell a story, and he leaves lots of issues unresolved. One of Lewis's good friends, the poet Ruth Pitter, once challenged him about how the Beaver family in *The Lion, the Witch and the Wardrobe* managed to serve up potatoes for their meal with the children. Surely the Narnian winter would have prevented these from growing! And what about the oranges and sugar that would be needed for the marmalade roll that followed the potatoes? Where did they come from?

Yes, there are inconsistencies within individual novels of the Chronicles of Narnia, as well as across the whole series. But so what? Lewis wasn't writing a scholarly article; he was penning a story, designed to delight its readers and open up some deeper themes.

So what themes did Lewis open up with the Chronicles of Narnia? Let's look at one of the most important – the issue of which story (and which storyteller) we can trust.

Which Story Can We Trust?

Lewis wanted us to understand that we live in a world that is shaped by stories – by narratives which tell us who we are and what really matters. But which story can we trust? One of the dominant narratives of Western culture goes something like this: 'We are here by accident, meaningless products of a random process. We can only invent meaning and purpose in life, and do our best to stay alive – even though there is no point to life.' This is the narrative favoured by writers such as Jean-Paul Sartre and Richard Dawkins. But is it right? And should we trust those who tell this story?

There is another narrative, which takes a very different approach. 'We are precious creatures of a loving God, who has created us for something special that we are asked to do. We have the privilege of being able to do something good and useful for God in this world, and need to work out what it is.' This is the story we find in the Bible and echoed in great Christian writers down the ages.

These two stories are totally incompatible. They can't both be right. So which do we trust? One of Lewis's great achievements in Narnia is to help us understand that we live in a world of competing narratives. In the end, we have to decide for ourselves which is right. And having made that decision, we then need to inhabit the story we trust. Lewis helps us deal with both questions.

The first is very straightforward and easy to grasp. When the four children enter the world of Narnia in

The Lion, the Witch and the Wardrobe, they hear stories being told about this mysterious land. But which of them is right? Is Narnia *really* the realm of the White Witch? Or is she a usurper, whose power will be broken when two Sons of Adam and two Daughters of Eve sit on the four thrones at Cair Paravel? Is Narnia *really* the realm of the mysterious Aslan, whose return is expected at any time?

Gradually, one story about Narnia emerges as supremely plausible – the story of the great and noble lion, Aslan. Each individual story of Narnia turns out to be part of this greater narrative. *The Lion, the Witch and the Wardrobe* hints at (and partially discloses) the 'big picture', expanded in the remainder of the Narnia series. This 'grand narrative' of interlocking stories makes sense of the riddles the children see and experience around them. It allows the children to understand their experiences with a new clarity and depth, like a camera lens bringing a landscape into sharp focus.

The stories of Narnia seem childish nonsense to some. But to others, they are utterly transformative. For the latter group, these evocative stories affirm that it is possible for the weak and foolish to have a noble calling in a dark world; that our deepest intuitions point us to the true meaning of things; that there is indeed something beautiful and wonderful at the heart of the universe; and that this may be found, embraced and adored.

At the core of the Chronicles of Narnia lies Lewis's imaginative retelling of the Christian 'big story' or 'grand narrative' of creation, the fall, redemption and final consummation. A good and beautiful creation is spoiled and ruined by a fall, in which the Creator's power is denied and usurped. The Creator then enters into the creation to break the power of the usurper and restore things through a redemptive sacrifice. Yet even after the coming of the Redeemer, the struggle against sin and evil continues, and will not be ended until the final restoration and transformation of all things.

This brings us to the second point that Lewis makes so convincingly in the Chronicles of Narnia. The story of Aslan is not just something we hear about. We are invited to enter this story and become part of it. It's not an easy point to understand. Lewis wants us to see that our own story is given meaning, direction and purpose by the greater story of God. Let's try to unpack what Lewis means.

We each have our own unique story. But our own story needs to be brought into connection with a 'grand narrative', a 'big story' which gives our story a new importance and significance. Why? Because we realise that our story is part of something bigger. Our own story is framed by something greater, which gives us value and purpose. In one sense, faith is about embracing this bigger story and allowing our own story to become part of it.

Lewis's remarkable achievement in the Chronicles of Narnia is to allow his readers to inhabit this 'big story' – to get inside it and feel what it is like to be part of it. *Mere Christianity* allows us to understand Christian ideas; the Narnia stories allow us to step inside and *experience* the Christian story and judge it by its ability to make sense of things and 'chime in' with our deepest intuitions about truth, beauty and goodness. If the series is read in the order of publication, the reader enters this narrative in *The Lion, the Witch and the Wardrobe*, which concerns the coming – the 'advent' – of the Redeemer. *The Magician's Nephew* deals with the narrative of creation and the fall, while *The Last Battle* concerns the ending of the old order and the advent of a new creation.

The remaining four novels (*Prince Caspian, The Voyage of the Dawn Treader, The Horse and His Boy* and *The Silver Chair*) deal with the period between these two advents. Lewis here explores the life of faith, lived in the tension between the past and future comings of Aslan. Aslan is now at one and the same time an object of memory and of hope. Lewis speaks of an exquisite longing for Aslan when he cannot be seen clearly; of a robust yet gracious faith, able to withstand cynicism and scepticism; of people of character who walk trustingly through the shadowlands, seeing them 'in a mirror darkly', and learning to deal with a world in which they are assaulted by evil and doubt.

Lewis deftly shows how the stories of the individual children – particularly Lucy, who is in many ways the central human character of the series – become shaped by the story of Aslan. Lucy's love for Aslan is expressed in her commitment to him. She wants to do what he wants; she wants her story to reflect who he is. As a result, Lewis speaks of Lucy feeling 'lion-strength' flowing within her. She has become part of the story of Aslan. But – and this is a hugely important 'but' – she has not lost her own identity. Her story remains her own. However, her story now makes more sense because Lucy has gained a sense of value and meaning. By embracing the story of Aslan as central to *her* story, she has gained a new sense of identity and purpose.

Lewis here develops a New Testament theme which has a long history of exploration within the Christian faith. It is stated with particular clarity in Paul's letter to the Galatians: 'I have been crucified with Christ; and it is no longer I who live, but it is Christ who lives in me. And the life I now live in the flesh I live by faith in the Son of God, who loved me and gave himself for me' (Galatians 2:19–20). Faith involves putting to death the old self and rising to a new life. We do not lose our individuality; rather, we gain a new identity while still remaining individuals who are loved by God. In other words, we become new individuals without ceasing to be individuals.

Lewis reworks this theme in his Chronicles of Narnia. We stop defining our own frames of reference. We come to see that our individual stories can become traps, in which we become our own prisoners. We can get locked into ways of thinking and acting that are purely self-serving. Lucy and the other children realise that there is a 'bigger story' and long to become part of it. And they die to themselves, in that they relocate and recontextualise their own stories within this 'grand narrative'. They die to themselves, and live for Aslan. They surrender a self-centred story and replace it with an Aslan-centred story. Not only does this make more sense of things, it also gives them purpose, value and meaning.

There's much wisdom here, and we shall come back to these themes in our next meeting. But as this one comes to an end, Lewis might give us an example of how telling a story makes a theological idea more 'real' and intelligible than if we read about it in some introduction to Christian theology. With a twinkle in his eye, Lewis might tell us about the 'undragoning' of Eustace.

Images of Reality: The 'Undragoning' of Eustace Scrubb

Everyone has his or her own favourite novel in the Chronicles of Narnia. For me, it's *The Lion, the Witch and the Wardrobe*. Perhaps it's because this was the first of the novels I read. Or maybe it's the power of its narrative. But whatever the reasons may be, it's the Narnia novel I most enjoy reading. Yet many prefer *The Voyage of the Dawn Treader*. Why? Often it's because of one single episode: the 'undragoning' of Eustace Scrubb.

Lewis's opening line in *The Voyage of the Dawn Treader* is seen by many as one of its most memorable features: 'There was a boy called Eustace Clarence Scrubb, and he almost deserved it.' Eustace Scrubb is portrayed as a thoroughly unsympathetic character, whom Lewis develops as an example of selfishness. It's difficult to like him to begin with, and it's just as difficult to feel sorry for him when he changes into a dragon as a result of his 'greedy, dragonish thoughts'.

The thoroughly obnoxious Eustace encounters some enchanted gold. This will make him master of all! But instead, it masters him. Eustace is completely selfish and greedy in his thoughts and behaviour. His personal story is self-centred and self-absorbed. Lewis depicts him as becoming what he already is. But what has a dragon got to do with this narrative of greed?

Lewis loved old Norse mythology, and borrowed the image of a dragon from the Norse story about the greedy giant Fáfnir, who turned himself into a dragon to protect his ill-won gain. Lewis wants us to understand that the story of Eustace was one of self-centredness and self-absorption. In the end, he becomes trapped within his own story. And he cannot break free from it.

This is the point Lewis really wants to make. Having become a dragon, how does Eustace stop being one? Lewis presents Eustace's initial transformation into a dragon and his subsequent 'undragoning' as a double transformation that reveals both Eustace's selfish, fallen nature and the transforming power of divine grace.

The Voyage of the Dawn Treader provides a brilliant description of Eustace's realising, to his horror, that he has become a dragon. He doesn't like this at all and he frantically tries to scratch off his dragon's skin. However, each layer he removes merely reveals yet another layer of scales beneath it. He simply cannot break free from his prison. He is trapped within a dragon's skin because he has become a dragon.

But salvation lies at hand. Aslan appears, and tears away at the dragon flesh with his claws. The lion's claws cut so deeply that Eustace is in real pain – 'worse than anything I've ever felt'. And when the scales are finally removed, Aslan plunges the raw and bleeding Eustace into a well from which he emerges purified and renewed, with his humanity restored. The storyline is dramatic, realistic and shocking. But the power of the narrative brings home the Christian themes that Lewis believed could not be described as effectively through a series of well-intentioned theological lectures. And while Lewis drew his dragon imagery from Norse mythology, the story of the 'undragoning' draws on the rich ideas and imagery of the New Testament.

So what are we to learn from this powerful and shocking story, so realistically depicted? As the raw imagery of Aslan tearing at Eustace's flesh makes clear, Eustace has been trapped by forces over which he has no control. The one who would be master has instead been mastered. The dragon is a symbol, not so much of sin itself, as of the power of sin to entrap, captivate and imprison. It can be broken and mastered only by the Redeemer. Aslan is the one who heals and renews Eustace, restoring him to what he was intended to be.

The immersion in the water of the well is immediately familiar, picking up on the New Testament's language about baptism as dying to self and rising to Christ (see Romans 6). (The omission of this aspect of the 'undragoning' of Eustace in the recent film version of *The Voyage of the Dawn Treader* was one of the more irritating and unnecessary of its many weaknesses.)

Eustace is tossed into the well by Aslan, and emerges renewed and restored.

Reverting to the language of story, Lewis's point is that Eustace has become trapped in a web of falsehood and self-deceit. The story that promised riches and freedom has entrapped him. Eustace is so deeply enmeshed in this story that he cannot break free from its tissue of deception. Only Aslan can break the power of this story and enable Eustace to enter another story – where he really belongs.

And that answers the question of why stories are so important. The story we believe we are in determines what we think about ourselves and consequently how we live. For Lewis, Christianity doesn't just make sense of things. It changes our stories. It invites us to enter into, and be part of, a new story. And as Lewis has a lot more to say about this, we'll make sure we take this further next time we meet.

4

The Lord and the Lion: C.S. Lewis on Aslan and the Christian Life

'Aslan,' said Lucy, 'you're bigger.'
'That is because you are older, little one,' answered he.
'Not because you are?'
'I am not. But every year you grow, you will find me bigger.'

C.S. Lewis, *Prince Caspian*

Bonnie Tyler's hit 'Holding Out for a Hero' struck a deep chord with many people when it came out in 1984, especially its best-known line, 'I need a hero!' Whom do we look to for inspiration? Who is our role model? We need someone whom we can admire, and who can inspire us to become better people.

Lewis's deep knowledge of literature helped him reach the same conclusion. The great legends of King Arthur and the Knights of the Round Table were all about the quest for virtue. They were an inspiration in dark times. And Lewis went on to create his own hero – a very special lion called Aslan.

I was having lunch with some colleagues to talk about a lecture they wanted me to give in London. Their ten-year-old daughter joined us briefly, before we got on to the business part of the discussion. 'This is Professor McGrath,' they told her. 'He knows a lot about C.S. Lewis!'

The girl's eyes brightened. 'When you next see him, could you tell him I love Aslan? He's the most wonderful lion I know. I wish I could know him better.'

She's not alone. Just about everyone agrees that the noble lion Aslan, the standout character of the Chronicles of Narnia, is probably Lewis's greatest literary creation. Lewis seems to have begun to write *The Lion, the Witch and the Wardrobe* without any clear idea of how its plot and characters would develop. Then Aslan came 'bounding in' to Lewis's imagination, and the narrative took shape. Aslan 'pulled the whole story together, and soon He pulled the six other Narnian stories in after him'.[1] Although the process by which Lewis wrote the seven chronicles of Narnia remains unclear at points, there are good reasons for suggesting that once Lewis devised the central character, Aslan, the novels more or less wrote themselves.

So how did Aslan come 'bounding in' to Lewis's imagination? We can offer several pointers, even if none of them really explains everything. For a start, the image of a lion has played an important role in the Christian theological tradition as an image of Christ, building on the New Testament's reference to Christ as the 'Lion of the tribe of Judah, the Root of David' (Revelation 5:5).

And Lewis's close friend Charles Williams had written a novel titled *The Place of the Lion* (1931), which Lewis read with interest.

Furthermore, the lion is the traditional symbol associated with Lewis's childhood church, St Mark's Anglican Church in Dundela, in the Strandtown area of Belfast. The church's rectory, which Lewis visited regularly as a child, had a door knocker in the form of a lion's head. The use of the image of a lion is thus relatively easy to understand, even though Lewis's development of the idea goes way beyond any of these original ideas.

Aslan plays a pivotal role in Narnia, just as Jesus Christ is central to the Christian faith. Although Aslan is often described as an 'extended metaphor' for Jesus Christ, this depiction is unhelpful – not least because it completely fails to recognise the extraordinary power of presence that Aslan exercises within the Chronicles of Narnia, particularly *The Lion, the Witch and the Wardrobe*, *The Magician's Nephew* and *The Last Battle*. Aslan is no metaphor; he is a living figure who stands at the heart of Lewis's literary creation. We cannot treat Aslan simply as a symbol or a cipher for something else. We must respect him as a literary creation in his own right, appreciating him for what he *is*, in addition to reflecting on what he *suggests*.

Yet while we cannot simply identify Aslan with Christ, Lewis clearly intended us to see a relationship between them. Aslan helps us to think about Jesus Christ by engaging our imagination as much as by informing our reason. Lewis does not *tell* us what Jesus Christ is like; he *shows* us what Aslan is like and allows us to take things from there by ourselves. *We* have to make the connections. Aslan is a character of such imaginative and spiritual depth that many readers of Narnia find themselves drawn to him for reasons they find difficult to put into words. In one sense, Aslan is an imaginative surrogate for Jesus Christ, helping us begin a more serious engagement with the place of Christ in the Christian life.

There is no doubt that Aslan is to be seen as a 'Christ figure'. Lewis made it clear that this was a complex relationship, best framed in terms of a 'supposal': 'Let us *suppose* that there were a land like Narnia, and that the Son of God, as he became a Man in our world, became a Lion there, and then imagine what would happen.'[2]

So let's have lunch with Lewis and explore how the figure of Aslan opens up and illuminates some of the core themes of the Christian faith. Let's begin by looking at a classic objection. What if God is just an invention – something we dreamed up, in order to make life more meaningful and give us hope for the future? Lewis's response to this question is well worth considering. So, as we talk, we might ask Lewis to tell us more about this.

'A Bigger and Better Cat': Aslan and the Problem of Projection

Lewis might begin by telling us why he was an atheist as a younger man. One of the most important arguments for atheism was originally set out by the German philosopher

Ludwig Feuerbach in the 1840s and popularised in England in the later nineteenth century by the novelist George Eliot. For Feuerbach and Eliot, God was simply an invention. God was merely a projection of unfulfilled human longings, the invention of a restless and dissatisfied humanity. The most famous statement of this approach is that of the psychoanalyst Sigmund Freud, who declared that God was a 'wish-fulfilment'. God was just a copy of a human father. In his late work *The Future of an Illusion* (1927), Freud argued that God was a projection of the father figure that everyone craved, a fulfilment of the 'oldest, strongest, and most urgent wishes of mankind'.[3]

These views were widely and somewhat uncritically accepted in Western intellectual culture during the period between the two world wars. Indeed, their popularity was often taken as an indication of their truth. Christianity rested on an illusion that we create as a way of giving ourselves meaning and significance. God is nothing more than the projection of some kind of father figure onto an imaginary transcendent screen. Fathers are real enough – but God is simply an imagined father, whom we invent because we need security.

How could such an idea be countered? One way is to mount a logical attack on the approach. Suppose we do want God to exist. Why is that a reason for saying God *can't* exist? After all, one way of reading the Christian doctrine of creation points to a 'homing instinct' for God being planted within the human mind and heart. And what if atheism is also a wish-fulfilment? Historians point out that atheism became a significant force in Western culture partly because it meant that if we no longer have to reference God in our moral reasoning, we can do what we like.

Now, these arguments are important, and can easily be developed to undermine the force of the idea that God is simply some kind of 'projection' of the human heart. But, like all arguments, they are not very exciting. They engage the reason, but not the imagination. So how would Lewis, with his deft ability to bring reason and imagination together, deal with this question? To find the answer, we turn to *The Silver Chair*, one of the most interesting of the Chronicles of Narnia. Why is it so interesting? Because it reworks a famous image used by the ancient Greek philosopher Plato – a dark underground cave.

Plato asks us to imagine a group of people trapped in a cave, knowing only a world of flickering shadows cast by a fire. Since they don't have any experience of another world, they assume the shadows are the only reality. The cave is all there is. It defines the limits of reality. Yet we know – and are meant to know! – that there is another world beyond the cave, awaiting discovery.

When I first read this passage, I was an eighteen-year-old, hard-nosed rationalist who had yet to discover Christianity. I regarded Plato's analogy as typical escapist superstition. *What you see is what you get*, I thought, *and that's the end of the matter.* Yet a still, small voice within me whispered words of doubt. *What if this world is only part of the story? What if this world is only a shadowland? What if there is something more wonderful beyond it?* In *The Silver Chair*, Lewis uses Plato's analogy to make the case for Christianity, using a powerful imaginative argument.

The plot of *The Silver Chair* is a bit like a *Mission: Impossible* film. Puddleglum (a mildly depressed Marshwiggle), Jill Pole and Eustace Scrubb are sent to rescue a Narnian prince from his captivity. The prince is being held against his will by the queen of the Underworld in a dark subterranean cavern. After some exciting adventures, the heroes arrive in the underground world, where they meet the prince, who is tied to a chair. They cut his bonds and set him free.

Just as they are about to leave, the queen arrives. She throws some green powder on the fire and begins to play some beguiling music. The 'sweet and drowsy' fragrance of the burning powder and the 'steady, monotonous thrumming' of the music enchants them. They begin to lose their memory of the 'overworld' – the real world – beyond the dark cavern. We see here Lewis's brilliant evocation of cultural suppression of the deep human instinct that there is more to life than what we see around us. We need to break free from this 'evil enchantment'. For Lewis, the key lies as much in our imagination as in our reason.

Having beguiled her visitors, the queen tries to persuade them that they are deluded. There is no overworld. Her kingdom is the only reality. They have simply invented the idea of the overworld. The Narnian prince protests. There really is an overworld! It's not like this dark kingdom – it has a sun! The queen invites him to tell her more about this so-called 'sun'. Looking around, the prince sees a lamp. The sun is just like that lamp, he declares:

> You see that lamp. It is round and yellow and gives light to the whole room; and hangeth moreover from the roof. Now that thing which we call the sun is like the lamp, only far greater and brighter. It giveth light to the whole Overworld and hangeth in the sky.[4]

The queen laughs dismissively. There is no sun! The prince has simply invented the idea, based on the lamp. 'Your *sun* is a dream; and there is nothing in that dream that was not copied from the lamp. The lamp is the real thing; the *sun* is but a tale, a children's story.' Anyway, what does the sun hang from? This stumps the prince.

Jill now enters the conversation. What about Aslan? He's part of the real world outside the cave, isn't he? The queen ridicules Jill's intervention. Jill has merely invented this lion, just as the prince invented the sun. Aslan is simply a big imaginary cat, in the same way the sun is just an imaginary lamp. 'You've seen cats, and now you want a bigger and better cat, and it's to be called a *lion*.' Everything in their 'make-believe' world, the queen confidently assures them, has simply been copied from 'the real world, this world of mine, which is the only world'. They're deluded. It's time to face up to reality!

Finally, Puddleglum, Jill, Eustace and the Narnian prince are able to make their escape and get back to the real world – which they are reassured to find is not an illusion! Yet the important thing about this passage is not just the answer Lewis gives, but the way in which he gives it. Let's focus on his approach and appreciate its wisdom.

Lewis rebuts the 'projection' theory by *telling a story*. The appeal of his approach lies primarily with the imagination, not with reason. We grasp Lewis's point through our imaginations, and our reason struggles to keep up. In effect, Lewis's narrative subverts Freud's account of the origins of belief in God by showing that this seemingly sophisticated argument is actually rather shallow and superficial. How does he do this?

Lewis's readers know there is a sun. They can easily imagine the scenario of an underground realm (especially if they've read Plato, from whom Lewis borrowed this image). And they can just as easily imagine someone who has been imprisoned within this world all his or her life, who thinks that the underground kingdom is the only reality! They smile with amusement when this person declares that anyone who thinks there is a world beyond the cave is deluded. *Just who is deluded?* we wonder. Knowing the reality, we can smile at the superficial plausibility of the illusion. Lewis's appeal is to our imaginations. He helps us to *see* the weakness of this approach.

Lewis's point is that Feuerbach and Freud have cast a spell over Western culture, aiming to convince us that they are right and we are wrong. They present their speculative theories as if they were self-evident truths: *Only a fool would think there is a God!* Lewis helps us see that, in the first place, their approach is only a theory, and in the second, it is not a particularly plausible theory. It's only one way of looking at things – which is what the word *theory* really means – and there are other (and better) ways of seeing. Lewis's story gives us another way of looking at this 'projection' theory, which makes us realise that it is far more vulnerable than we might otherwise have realised.

Yet there is another point here, too easily overlooked. The narrative of *The Silver Chair* initially calls into question the existence of the overworld – and then of Aslan himself. When this is interpreted in Christian terms (as Lewis surely wished), this is initially a challenge to the existence of heaven, and then of Christ. It is important to remember here that Lewis's conversion to Christianity took place in two stages. In the first phase, Lewis came to believe in God, seeing this as linked with the existence of heaven, as a transcendent realm.[5] Second, a little later he began to believe in the divinity of Jesus Christ. The order of analysis in *The Silver Chair* parallels Lewis's own conversion story. Lewis initially defends the existence of a transcendent reality, and then the existence of Jesus Christ (here represented by Aslan).

We now need to look at Aslan more closely and explore how Lewis uses his most brilliant literary creation as a lens through which we can see Christ more clearly.

A Person, Not an Idea

The most characteristic feature of Lewis's depiction of Aslan is that he is a figure who evokes awe and wonder. Lewis develops this theme by emphasising that Aslan is *wild* – an awe-inspiring, magnificent creature who has not been tamed through domestication, or had his claws pulled out to ensure he is powerless. As the Beaver whispered to the children, 'He's wild, you know. Not like a *tame* lion.'[6]

Lewis's telling phrase is much more important than many realise. Aslan is not a '*tame*' lion'. Throughout the Chronicles of Narnia, Aslan is portrayed as a magnificent living animal, who has a profound effect on those he meets. When Aslan's name is mentioned for the first time, the four children feel 'quite different'. Yet each experiences different reactions. Edmund feels 'mysterious horror', Peter feels 'brave and adventurous', Susan feels elated, and Lucy gets the feeling you have when you 'realise it is the beginning of the holidays'.[7]

There is clearly something special about Aslan. Yet each of the children experiences this in his or her own way. Lewis's narrative constantly emphasises that Aslan encounters and transforms people individually. It is impossible to miss Lewis's allusions to the Gospel narratives about the encounters between Jesus Christ and individuals – such as his meetings with Zacchaeus and the woman at the well. They come away from those encounters as different people. Their world has been turned upside down by the stranger who seems to know everything about them.

Lewis was concerned about two trends that he discerned within the Christian churches of his day, each of which seemed to impoverish the majesty and mystery of Christ. First, there was the well-meaning preacher who tried to make Christ more accessible by using homely analogies – for example, 'Jesus as our friend'. Yet this amiable analogy is all too easily misunderstood as 'Jesus is *just* our friend'.

A major theme in Lewis's philosophy of education is that we must expand our vision so that it is better able to take in reality, rather than limit reality to what we can cope with. Lewis makes this point repeatedly in the Chronicles of Narnia. Aslan overwhelms the children's ability to understand him. They simply *cannot* take him in. No matter how hard they try, they are able to grasp only so much of his nature and purposes. Aslan is good, but he is not tame. They learn to respect and trust him, even though they know they do not fully understand him.

Lewis's second concern was with theologians who reduced Jesus Christ to neat little doctrinal formulas. Lewis didn't have problems with theological statements about Jesus Christ – for example, the traditional credal declaration that he is 'true God'. What he was worried about was that these formulas might become substitutes for the living reality of Jesus Christ.

In the Chronicles of Narnia, Lewis set out the story of Aslan as a retelling of the 'actual incarnation, crucifixion, and resurrection'. The reader is invited to reflect on this story and draw conclusions about Aslan's true identity and significance. Indeed, Lewis offers generous hints and guidance about what those conclusions might be throughout his narrative. But Lewis's *emphasis* is on the story; the interpretation arises from the story and is secondary to it. This does not mean that the interpretation is unimportant. It is part of this overall picture – but only part of it. Lewis wants us to see that Aslan should be appreciated as a totality, not simply reduced to a mere theory. We see here Lewis's characteristic appeal to both reason and imagination. He invites us to 'see' Aslan fully.

Lewis needs to be heard here. Much Christian thinking about Jesus Christ has been influenced by what scholars call the 'Enlightenment project' – a rationalist approach to faith and theology originating primarily in the eighteenth century. One leading theme of this rationalist culture of the eighteenth century was its attempt to master the world by reducing it to theory. Enlightenment rationalism encouraged the idea that reality be reduced to something that reason could master – in other words, theories. As a result, both God and Jesus Christ were often reduced to what human reason could manage. Both God and Christ came to be trapped within rationalist cages, like majestic tigers imprisoned and unable to show themselves for what they really were.

Lewis protests against this trend, not least in relation to the core realities of the Christian faith. Perhaps Lewis's conversion experience, in which he realised that God was drawing close to him, encouraged him to reject impoverished ideas of God. For Lewis, theory was determined and limited by reality. For many modernists, however, reality was determined and limited by theory. One of Lewis's most distinctive themes concerns the secondary nature of Christian doctrines. These, he argues, are 'translations into our *concepts* and *ideas* of that [which] God has already expressed in a language more adequate' – namely, the 'grand narrative' of the Christian faith itself.[8]

Thus Lewis argues that 'the theories are not themselves the thing you are asked to accept'.[9] Theories are only intermediaries for an encounter with reality, offering partial and reduced rather than total and comprehensive accounts of what they depict. These second-order levels of engagement with reality may be neat, crisp and admirably logical. Yet they fall short of what true Christianity is all about – an encounter with the living God, something that can never be accommodated without radical imaginative loss. A God who is reduced to what reason can cope with is not a God who can be worshipped.

So there's a sense in which Lewis is telling us that there are limits to our *understanding* of Jesus Christ. It's too easy to imprison Jesus Christ within a theological cage, taming him and mastering him. Lewis reminds us that Christ masters us, and that part of our discipleship of the mind is to expand our intellectual vision and range so that we can appreciate him more fully.

Yet the Christian life is about more than just sorting out our ideas. It's about the way we live. Let's ask Lewis to tell us about how the Narnia novels help us think about virtue.

Lewis on Virtue: How Do We Become Good People?

If the Chronicles of Narnia are read in the order of publication,[10] the reader first encounters Aslan in *The Lion, the Witch and the Wardrobe*, which deals with the coming of salvation. *The Magician's Nephew* deals with the great themes of creation and the fall, while *The Last Battle* concerns the ending of the old order and the dawn of a new creation. In every case, Aslan is of central importance, mirroring the roles of Jesus Christ as Creator, Redeemer and Judge.

The other four novels (*Prince Caspian, The Voyage of the Dawn Treader, The Horse and His Boy* and *The Silver Chair*) reflect on the life of faith, which is framed in terms of the past and future comings of Aslan. As I mentioned previously, Aslan is at one and the same time an object of memory and of hope. The characters in the story must walk through the 'shadowlands', the difficult place between remembrance and hope, where they are assaulted by evil and by doubt. They must fix their gaze upon Aslan. And it is in this context that Lewis explores how Aslan shapes the life of faith.

Christianity is about the way we behave, not just the way we think. One of Lewis's four series of broadcasts on the BBC during the Second World War dealt with the topic of 'Christian behaviour'. Throughout his letters, Lewis shows himself as someone who wanted to do what was right and to learn from others who could help him.

Perhaps we ought not to be surprised that a major theme in the Chronicles of Narnia is how we become – and remain! – good people. Gilbert Meilander, one of America's leading moral philosophers, pointed out how the Narnia novels are more than 'good stories'. They help us to 'build character' by providing us with examples from which we can learn, rather like an apprentice working with a master.[11]

Lewis realised that it isn't enough to tell people to be 'good'. They need someone to show them what goodness looks like. A role model is worth a thousand words! It's much better to tell a story which shows us how someone acted nobly than to read a textbook about the abstract idea of nobility.

The Chronicles of Narnia are packed full of stories. Some of them model good behaviour; some model bad. Yet we can learn from both. It is not simply a question of avoiding evil and embracing virtue. It is about recognising that we need to look hard at ourselves and realise that we have to face up to sometimes difficult and awkward truths. Seeking virtue is indeed noble. But there is some remedial work that we need to take care of before we begin the quest for virtue.

Self-knowledge has always been an important theme in Christian spirituality. It was important for Lewis as well. While writing my biography of Lewis, I frequently found myself concerned about his behaviour in the 1910s and 1920s. Lewis regularly lied to his father about his financial situation and his relationship with Mrs Moore, and felt no remorse about doing so. Deception seemed to come easily to Lewis, especially in his relationship with his father. Yet Lewis's conversion in 1930 changed everything. He began to deal with his own darker side. He realised that he was self-obsessed, and stopped keeping a diary. Most significantly, Lewis came to regret his behaviour towards his father. He realised he had acted unforgivably.

Owen Barfield, one of Lewis's closest friends, once remarked that the mature Lewis came to understand 'self-knowledge' as a 'recognition of his own weaknesses and shortcomings'.[12] Perhaps we should not be surprised that this is a major theme in the Chronicles of Narnia. For Lewis, one of Aslan's chief roles is to enable people to discover the truth about themselves. Aslan is such a commanding figure that he helps people who might otherwise remain locked in self-deception break free from this prison. Somehow, Aslan makes it possible for people to confront the truth about themselves.

Let's look at a familiar example to see what Lewis has in mind. In *The Magician's Nephew*, things take a turn for the worse when someone wakes nasty Queen Jadis up from her enchanted sleep. (Realising that she was unable to exert her evil influence for the time being, she had cast a spell of enchanted sleep on herself, leaving a bell nearby so that she could be aroused when the right moment came.) But who would do such a stupid thing? Who would be mad enough to unleash her evil?

When questioned by Aslan, Digory reluctantly admits that he was the one who rang the bell. He offers some half-hearted defence of his action. But as Aslan stares at him, Digory breaks down and admits his failure. He abandons his pathetic attempt at self-justification and takes responsibility for his actions. The gaze of Aslan compels him to tell the truth – both to Aslan and to himself. It is as if Aslan offers a mirror in which we see ourselves as we really are. Or a light which reveals what we are *really* like, no matter how uncomfortable this may be.

Lewis is trying to help us realise that the quest for virtue involves both breaking the power of sin and embracing the power of good. Both, for Lewis, require the grace of God. It is no accident that Lewis portrays Aslan as someone who is *inspirational*. There is something about him that enables us to see and do things that otherwise would lie beyond our ability or inclination. A rich theology of divine grace nestles within the stories of Aslan's encounters with people (such as Digory) and with the other inhabitants of Narnia.

Lewis here develops a theme often found in the long tradition of Christian spiritual writing, which holds that it is by contemplating Christ that we are enabled to identify and confront our sin and resolve to become better people. Yet this is not clumsily forced on the readers of the Chronicles of Narnia. There are points where the imagery is obvious to those in the know. For example, the deeply moving account of Susan and Lucy stroking the dead Aslan's fur in *The Lion, the Witch and the Wardrobe* evokes the medieval imagery of the *Pietà* – Michelangelo's depiction of Mary holding the dead body of Jesus Christ, immediately following the crucifixion. Yet Lewis's story makes the point effectively for all his readers, even if it is his Christian readers who will appreciate it to the full. We need help if we are to stop doing wrong and start being good.

So what of virtue? As a scholar of both the classics and medieval literature, Lewis knew the importance of the quest for the good life. It is a theme that recurs throughout both Lewis's Chronicles of Narnia and J.R.R. Tolkien's *The Lord of the Rings*. Both show the need for people of character and virtue in a complex and confusing world. Good does not triumph unless good people rise to the challenges around them.

Both Lewis and Tolkien show how it is often the weak and lowly who are called upon to undertake great challenges. Tolkien brings this out in the critical role of the lowly hobbits in securing and destroying the malignant ring. Lewis shows us how the humble and lowly can achieve greatness in one of his most beloved characters – Reepicheep the mouse.

Reepicheep is a small mouse who realises that he has a great calling, even if he does not fully understand it. In *Prince Caspian* he is brave and courteous; in *The Voyage of the Dawn Treader* he develops a passion for achieving the task to which he has been called. His concern is not to win glory or fame for himself, but to fulfil his quest – to travel to the 'Utter East' and find 'Aslan's Country'.

Reepicheep is clearly modelled on a medieval knight – a noble and chivalrous 'warrior mouse',[13] bringing together valour and purity. Lewis is trying to help us see that Reepicheep does not act bravely and nobly only every now and then. His point is that Reepicheep has become a brave and noble mouse, and that this shapes all his judgements and actions. Who Reepicheep *is* determines what Reepicheep *does*.

Lewis opens up the great question of how we pursue virtue in his own helpful way – not by giving us lectures on moral philosophy (though let's remember that Lewis's first lectures at Oxford were on this theme!), but by telling us stories in which we can see virtue in action. He shows us what virtue looks like and helps us understand how we become virtuous.

And whether directly or indirectly, Aslan lies at the heart of all these stories of virtue. He is their ultimate inspiration. He invites others to become part of his story. It is a privilege to become part of this story, and that privilege carries with it responsibilities. We are called on to work out what our roles should be and how we should behave appropriately. By giving us role models in the Chronicles of Narnia, Lewis allows us to grasp how even humble people can become noble and virtuous and make a difference in the greater scheme of things.

That's why exploring Lewis's literary creations in the Narnia series is so useful when seeking the answers to the meaning-of-life questions – whether a question is what the true nature of God is or how we become good people. Through the Narnia series, Lewis shows these truths to us instead of telling us about them. This approach made Lewis one of the most beloved Christian authors of the twentieth century.

Lewis would probably be pleased that this is the last time we'll raise the topic of Narnia with him. His correspondence suggests that he found it a little tiring discussing its many themes with people, each of whom demanded his personal attention! In our next imagined meeting with Lewis, we'll move on to discuss the discipline which he made his own – apologetics.

5

Talking about Faith:
C.S. Lewis on the Art of Apologetics

What we believe always remains intellectually possible; it never becomes intellectually compulsive. I have an idea that when this ceases to be so, the world will be ending.

C.S. Lewis, 'Religion and Rocketry'

One thing our imagined meetings with Lewis cannot convey is Lewis's voice. We can get a sense of his *literary* voice through his many written works, but what was Lewis like to *listen* to?

I have received lots of letters from people telling me about their experiences of hearing Lewis lecture. Some remembered his days at Cambridge, when he would walk into a lecture theatre, still wearing his hat and scarf, and begin delivering his lecture as he walked to the podium. Another letter was especially interesting. It was from someone who had been an undergraduate at Oxford during the Second World War and had heard Lewis speak about the Christian faith one evening. 'The atmosphere was electric,' he told me. 'My friends and I were all ready to repent and be baptised, right there and then!'

Lewis's impassioned speeches and writings on the Christian faith have earned him a reputation as one of the greatest Christian apologists of all time. When he began his studies at Oxford University in January 1919, Lewis hoped to be remembered as an atheist poet – someone who destroyed the plausibility of God through his verbal eloquence and the power of argument. Yet in the end, it was the plausibility of a dull and joyless atheism that crumbled before him.

So what brought about the change? How did Lewis move from an angry opponent of the Christian faith to a convincing apologist for it? We can identify two major influences on Lewis's growing interest in Christianity and increasing appreciation of its rational and imaginative appeal. First, his friends – such as Owen Barfield – raised questions about his atheism that Lewis knew couldn't be answered. Second, Lewis read works by Christian writers – such as G.K. Chesterton – which helped him to realise that their faith provided a rich and realistic way of seeing, understanding and experiencing the world. None of these people made Christianity attractive for Lewis. They just helped him to grasp its fullness and depth.

Lewis was an apologist who was helped to come to faith by other apologists, such as Chesterton. Lewis asked tough questions about faith and God, and the answers he came to on his own were not satisfactory. He needed others' help to remove his barriers to belief. And

Lewis's chain of apologists needs to be kept going. Many Christians regard Lewis as having played a major role in bringing them to faith. So what are they doing to help others to come to faith? Are they doing for others what Lewis did for them?

Lewis would leave us in no doubt of the urgency of the apologetic task. It needs to be done! And done *well*. While there is no doubt a place for 'professional' apologists, it's a task that all believers must share. Lewis would want us to learn the lessons that he learned the hard way – by trial and error.

So let's imagine that Lewis is giving us a tutorial on apologetics. What would he tell us? But perhaps we need to begin by reflecting on just what we mean when we talk about 'apologetics'. It's not a word we use much in everyday conversation. The term *apologetics* makes a lot more sense when we consider the meaning of the Greek word on which it is based – *apologia*. An *apologia* is a 'defence' – a reasoned case which proves the innocence of an accused person in court, or demonstrates the truth of an argument or belief. We find this term used in the New Testament – as in 1 Peter 3:15–16, which many see as a classic biblical statement of the importance of apologetics:

> In your hearts sanctify Christ as Lord. Always be ready to make your defence [*apologia*] to anyone who demands from you an accounting [*logos*] for the hope that is in you; yet do this with gentleness and reverence.

The three main tasks of apologetics could be framed in terms of defending, commending and translating our faith.

1. *Defending.* Here the apologist tries to work out what stops people from believing. Have these obstacles arisen through misunderstandings or misrepresentations? If so, these need to be corrected. Have they arisen because of a genuine difficulty over Christian truth claims? If so, these need to be addressed. Lewis himself, as a former atheist, had a very good understanding of what prevented people from believing, and worked out good responses to each of these concerns – concerns he once took seriously himself.

2. *Commending.* Here the apologist sets out to allow the truth and relevance of the gospel to be appreciated. The gospel does not need to be made relevant to these audiences. The question concerns how we help the audience to grasp this relevance – for example, by using helpful illustrations, analogies or stories to allow them to connect with it. Lewis proved to be a master of this process, and there is much to be learned from him.

3. *Translating.* Here the apologist recognises that many of the core ideas and themes of the Christian faith are likely to be unfamiliar. They need to be explained using familiar or accessible images, terms or stories. Through experience, Lewis worked out how he could faithfully and effectively communicate the

Christian faith to a culture which was having difficulty in understanding traditional Christian terms and ideas.

We have already told the story of how Lewis became the 'most dejected and reluctant convert in all England'.[1] But there are many Christian converts, of whom few become apologists. So what made Lewis become an apologist? How did he go about doing apologetics? And what might we learn from him as we attempt to defend, commend and translate our faith? Let's have our tutorial with Lewis and find out.

How Lewis Became an Apologist

In the summer of 1932, Lewis wrote his first book – *The Pilgrim's Regress*. It is a difficult work, partly because Lewis had yet to develop his characteristically fluid writing style. *The Pilgrim's Regress* is an attempt to explain how Lewis came to faith and the various obstacles he encountered along the way. Yet it is not really a work of apologetics. It is more an explanation of Lewis's own journey to faith, rather than an attempt to defend or commend the Christian faith.

Perhaps Lewis would never have taken on the mantle of an apologist had he not received an invitation to write a book on how Christians respond to suffering. In 1939 Ashley Sampson, the proprietor of a small London publishing imprint, asked Lewis if he would contribute a volume to a series of books Sampson had edited. The Christian Challenge series was intended to help people outside the Church to make more sense of what Christianity was all about. It brought together some leading Christian voices – such as John Kenneth Mozley, whose 1937 volume, *The Doctrine of the Incarnation*, was particularly well received – on major Christian themes.

Sampson wrote to Lewis, asking if he would be willing to write on the question of suffering. The topic and title were not up for discussion.[2] Lewis suggested that he write anonymously, as he did not feel entirely qualified to write on the topic. However, he had clearly come to the conclusion that since his conversion, he was called to explain the basics of faith to those outside the faith. He accepted the invitation. It was the first work of Christian apologetics that Lewis wrote. It was so well received that he went on to write others.

What Lewis has to say about suffering remains important and deserves a tutorial all to itself! But in this tutorial, we'll look at the methods Lewis developed of communicating and defending the Christian faith in an increasingly hostile cultural environment. Why was he so successful?

One obvious answer is that Lewis was both a very good speaker and a very good writer. Some good writers are terrible speakers. While this is an important point, it is not particularly helpful. Lewis might well encourage us to become good at writing and speaking, but these are not transferable skills! Yet Lewis *can* help us in terms of the approaches we adopt and the content of what we say or write. So let's begin by looking at one of his big themes – the need to learn and use the vocabulary of our audiences.

Translating into the Cultural Vernacular

Lewis was an Oxford academic. By the late 1930s, he had figured out how to lecture to England's brightest undergraduates and write learned papers and books that would cement his academic reputation. He was able to communicate effectively with an academic audience. But this was a very small audience! What about ordinary churchgoers? What about the British public at large – the kind of person who would listen to the radio in the 1940s? Lewis had no familiarity with this audience at all. He would have bombed, had he tried to speak to them.

But something unexpected happened. When the Second World War broke out, many senior clergy were concerned with ensuring that the British armed forces had access to Christian teaching and encouragement. W.R. Matthews, dean of St Paul's Cathedral, London, proposed that Lewis be invited to tour Royal Air Force bases and talk to the aircrews about his faith. It would have been a major challenge for Lewis, who was used to teaching some of the best university students in Britain. How would he cope with 'plodders' – young men who had left school at sixteen and had no intention of doing anything even remotely academic? Yet whatever misgivings he may have had, Lewis accepted the offer. It was a brilliant move. It provided Lewis with a platform that forced him to translate his ideas into 'uneducated language'.

His first lecture was at an air force base near Abingdon, just south of Oxford, in May 1941. Lewis thought it was a disaster. Nobody else did. They asked him for more. And more. We can imagine Lewis engaged in discussion and debate with hard-nosed, no-nonsense, tough-talking aircrews, learning how his academic style did not connect with them – and determining to do something about it. It was not long before Lewis was able to figure out how to express himself so that he could connect with this new audience.

By the end of the Second World War, Lewis was firmly established as one of the most effective popular speakers on Christianity, attracting huge radio audiences for his series of talks on Christianity. Nor was his success limited to speaking. Lewis was able to adapt his new skill to writing as well. *The Pilgrim's Regress* (1933) was clunky and ponderous. *The Screwtape Letters* (1942), however, showed off Lewis's new skills as a communicator – his winsome, engaging and witty prose – and won him a huge readership.

So what lessons did Lewis learn? And how can we learn from his success? Happily, Lewis gave a lecture on exactly this topic to clergy and youth leaders in Wales in 1945, in which he explained something about the insights and wisdom that he had to learn the hard way. Lewis would hammer home two points during our tutorial.

First, he would insist that we discover how ordinary people speak: 'We must learn the language of our audience.'[3] And how are we to do this? 'You have to find out by experience.'

Lewis is asking us to listen before we speak. We need to work out what words people use, the ideas that they find helpful, and the analogies and stories that connect with them. Then we need to weave these into what we say.

Second, having learned the language of our audience, we need to translate what we want to say into that language. As Lewis put it, we need to 'translate every bit of [our] Theology into the vernacular'.[4] This is not easy, Lewis concedes. But it is essential. Not only does it ensure that we can connect with our audiences. It also means that we have understood our own ideas. If we can't translate our thoughts into ordinary language, Lewis playfully suggests, then our thoughts are confused. 'Power to translate is the test of having really understood one's own meaning.'

So what kind of translation does Lewis have in mind? First, he's asking us to explain what technical words mean. We need to unpack words such as *incarnation* and *atonement*, using ordinary language to help people appreciate what they mean. But second, he's inviting us to use other genres to open these terms up. We could tell a story to unpack the doctrine of the incarnation – as Lewis himself did so effectively in *The Lion, the Witch and the Wardrobe.* Indeed, many Lewis scholars would argue that Lewis presents Christianity in a form that appeals to reason in *Mere Christianity* and in a form that appeals to the imagination in *The Lion, the Witch and the Wardrobe*. There's more to it than that, but this helps us work out what he had in mind.

Lewis himself was brilliant at appealing to the imagination, spicing up his famous wartime Broadcast Talks with neat illustrations and analogies that helped him to make his points. The great lecture theatres of Oxford demanded one way of communicating – a technique that Lewis had mastered. Popular communication demanded something rather different. And Lewis mastered this as well. He was 'bilingual' in that he could say the same thing in one way to one audience, and in another way to a different audience.

Reflecting on Mere Christianity

Polls suggest that Lewis's *Mere Christianity*, published in 1952, was one of the most influential and respected Christian books of the twentieth century. It has been enormously influential in bringing some to faith and in sustaining the faith of others. The book is basically an edited version of the four series of talks that Lewis gave for the BBC during the Second World War. These talks, which had been highly successful, now found a new audience. Let's look at this classic work and see what we can learn from it.

In preparing for these talks, Lewis went to considerable trouble to 'learn the language of his audience'. These talks were not an academic speaking down to his listeners, using words they could not understand about things that did not interest them. Lewis spoke with clarity and conviction. To put it simply: Lewis connected with his audience – both in the original radio talks and subsequently in *Mere Christianity*. Each chapter of *Mere Christianity* is short and self-contained, just like the original talks.

Yet what Lewis presented in *Mere Christianity* was not a hodgepodge of arguments about faith. As Lewis's Oxford colleague Austin Farrer perceptively remarked, Lewis makes us 'think we are listening to an argument', when in reality 'we are presented with a vision, and it is the vision that carries conviction'.[5] This vision appeals to the human longing for truth, beauty and goodness. Lewis's achievement is to show that what we observe and experience 'fits in' with the idea of God.

As we discussed in our first conversation with Lewis, he saw Christianity as the 'big picture' which weaves together the strands of experience and observation into a compelling pattern. The first part of *Mere Christianity* is titled 'Right and Wrong as a Clue to the Meaning of the Universe'. It is important to note the carefully chosen term *clue*. What Lewis is noting is that the world is emblazoned with such clues, none of which proves anything individually, but which taken together give a cumulative case for believing in God. These clues are the threads that make up the great pattern of the universe.

Mere Christianity begins with an invitation to reflect on two people having a dispute. Lewis argues that determining who is right and who is wrong depends on recognising some standard which both parties agree is binding and authoritative. Lewis makes the case that we are all aware of an objective standard to which we appeal and which we expect others to observe, a 'real law which we did not invent, and which we know we ought to obey'.[6]

Yet although everyone knows about this law, everyone still fails to live up to it. Lewis thus suggests that 'the foundation of all clear thinking about ourselves and the universe we live in' consists in our knowledge of a moral law and an awareness of our failure to observe it.[7] This awareness ought to 'arouse our suspicions' that there 'is Something which is directing the universe, and which appears in me as a law urging me to do right and making me feel responsible and uncomfortable when I do wrong'.[8] Lewis suggests that this points to an ordering mind governing the universe – which fits comfortably with the Christian idea of God.

The second line of argument concerns our experience of longing. It is an approach that Lewis had earlier developed in his sermon 'The Weight of Glory', preached at Oxford in 1941. Lewis reworked this argument for the purposes of his Broadcast Talks, making it much easier to understand. His argument can be summarised like this: we all long for something, only to find our hopes dashed and frustrated when we actually achieve or attain it. So how is this common human experience to be interpreted? Lewis argues that these earthly longings are 'only a kind of copy, or echo, or mirage' of our true homeland.[9] He develops an 'argument from desire', suggesting that every natural desire has a corresponding object and is satisfied only when this object is attained or experienced. This natural desire for transcendent fulfilment cannot be attained through anything in the present world, leading to the suggestion that it could be satisfied beyond the present world, in a world towards which the present order of things points.

Lewis argues that the Christian faith interprets this longing as a clue to the true goal of human nature. God is the ultimate end of the human soul, the sole source of human happiness and joy. Just as physical hunger points to a real human need which can be met through food, so this spiritual hunger corresponds to a real need which can be met through God. 'If I find in myself a desire which no experience in this world can satisfy, the most probable explanation is that I was made for another world.' Most people, Lewis argues, are aware of a deep sense of longing within themselves which cannot be satisfied by anything transient or created. Like right and wrong, this sense of longing is thus a clue to the meaning of the universe.

In his arguments from both morality and desire, Lewis appeals to the capacity of Christianity to 'fit' what we observe and experience. This is integral to Lewis's approach to apologetics, precisely because Lewis himself found it so persuasive and helpful a tool for making sense of things. The Christian faith provides a map that is found to fit in well with what we observe around us and experience within us. Again, perhaps this approach is expressed most succinctly in the famous quote from a wartime talk Lewis gave to the Socratic Club in Oxford: 'I believe in Christianity as I believe that the sun has risen – not just because I see it, but because by it, I see everything else.'[10]

For Lewis, the kind of 'sense making' offered by the Christian vision of reality is about discerning a resonance between the theory and the way the world seems to be. Though Lewis uses surprisingly few musical analogies in his published writings, his approach could be described as enabling the believer to hear the harmonics of the cosmos and to realise that it fits together *aesthetically* – even if there are a few logical loose ends that still need to be tied up.

So do Lewis's arguments in *Mere Christianity* still work? Some, it must be said, are showing their age, especially when Lewis makes assumptions about the moral values of his age. Yet his approaches still work remarkably well, raising questions about the deeper meaning of life that continue to speak to many – but not all – today. Both Lewis's 'argument from morality' and his 'argument from desire' continue to speak deeply, even if we might need to rephrase them and adapt their imagery to our own day and age. Lewis continues to evoke a sense of intrigue, interest and even wistfulness on the part of many of his readers.

Perhaps one of the lessons that we can learn from our tutorial with Lewis is that apologetics is at its best when it makes people wish that Christianity were true – by showing them its power to excite the imagination, to make sense of things and to bring stability, security and meaning to life. The final stage is to show people that it *is* true!

Reason in Apologetics

As we noted earlier, Lewis was an atheist himself while a student at Oxford University. His move away from atheism, initially to theism and then to Christianity, partly reflected his growing disenchantment with the imaginative deficiency of a godless world. It was dull and drab. He found that the 'glib and shallow rationalism' he had adopted was intellectually unpersuasive and existentially unsatisfying.

Lewis believed that Christianity was reasonable. He also believed that reason could not fully grasp the richness of the Christian faith. In 1926, while beginning to move away from atheism, Lewis commented to a friend that he was now convinced that reason was 'utterly inadequate to the richness and spirituality of real things'.[11] What really mattered lay beyond reason's ability to grasp it – even if it proved to be eminently reasonable once it was grasped. Does Lewis contradict himself here? Surely not. The point Lewis is making is that there are limits to what we can work out about the meaning of life for ourselves. He's right. Let me try to explain.

When I was young, I was very interested in astronomy. I had a little telescope, and enjoyed looking at the moons of the planet Jupiter and watching the slow movements of the planets against the background of the stars. Once I tracked the movement of the planet Mars for a period of weeks. I couldn't make sense of what I was seeing. Mars drifted eastwards for several nights, then seemed to stop and move westwards. Eventually, it moved eastwards again.[12] I was baffled.

Having completely failed to make sense of this, I asked my science teacher to explain it to me. He drew some diagrams to show me the relative motions of the earth and Mars. It was all about the earth rotating round the sun faster than Mars. After about five minutes, I got it. I could see what was happening. The penny had dropped. *But someone had to tell me.* My teacher gave me a framework for understanding what I had seen, and it made perfect sense. I couldn't figure it out for myself, but when someone wiser than me explained it, I could see it with clarity.

That's the point Lewis is trying to make. Christianity gives us a 'big picture' that we couldn't figure out for ourselves. But once we are given it, we discover just how much sense it makes. When Lewis tells us that faith is both 'beyond reason' and 'reasonable', he means that we need to be *told* and *shown* the way things really are. Yet once we have been given this way of seeing things, we discover just how much sense it makes.

Lewis developed approaches to apologetics based on an appeal to reason during the 1940s and early 1950s. Both *Miracles* and *Mere Christianity* argue that the Christian faith makes more sense of things than its eligious or secular alternatives.

Lewis was quite clear that reason was unable to *prove* the fundamental beliefs of the Christian faith. But it could nevertheless point us in the right direction. Especially in *Mere Christianity*, Lewis's concern was to explore what could be worked out about God 'on our own steam', instead of 'taking anything from the Bible or the Churches'.[13] Lewis wanted to be able to mount a public demonstration of the reasonableness of Christianity without appealing to any specifically Christian resources. Instead, he draws on common human experience and reflection about the world. Lewis's approach is to show how intelligent reflection on the experiences of life strongly *suggests* – but does not *prove* – that there is a God.

To demonstrate the reasonableness of faith does not mean proving every article of Christian belief. Rather, it means showing that there are good grounds that these beliefs are trustworthy and reliable. For Lewis, the Christian faith makes sense of what we observe and experience, even if it cannot offer unassailable and incorrigible proof of its truths.

So why does Lewis think this is important? He wants to sweep away a series of roadblocks to faith – one of which is the belief that faith is irrational. This was a big issue back in Lewis's day, and it remains so today. In the 2000s, the movement known as the 'New Atheism' rose briefly to prominence. This aggressive godlessness argues that religious belief is irrational and dangerous. Belief in God is about running away from reality, this 'New Atheism' holds, and about seeking refuge in toxic delusions that warp people's minds and make them do bad things. Lewis rightly sees that the rationality of belief in God has to be proclaimed and defended in both private and public.

Lewis's point is fair. Christians can't just tell *one another* that their faith makes sense. They've got to get that message over to their culture at large. For Lewis, apologetics thus aims to create and sustain 'an intellectual (and imaginative) climate favourable to Christianity'.[14] If we fail to do so, we will lose public credibility.

> If the intellectual climate is such that, when a man comes to the crisis at which he must accept or reject Christ, his reason and imagination are not on the wrong side, then his conflict will be fought out under favourable conditions. Those who help to produce and spread such a climate are therefore doing useful work.[15]

Much the same point was made more clearly by Lewis's close friend, the Oxford theologian and New Testament scholar Austin Farrer. In an article reflecting on why Lewis was so successful as an apologist, Farrer pointed out that demonstrating the reasonableness of faith was vital in securing its cultural acceptance.

> Though argument does not create conviction, the lack of it destroys belief. What seems to be proved may not be embraced; but what no one shows the ability to defend is quickly abandoned. Rational argument does

not create belief, but it maintains a climate in which belief may flourish.[16]

Lewis enriches our vision of apologetics, allowing us to affirm that Christianity makes sense, without limiting it to the 'glib and shallow' rationalism that he himself once knew as an atheist. Reason and imagination are woven together, using a rich concept of truth which emphasises how we come to *see* things properly and grasp their inner coherence. Truth, beauty and goodness all have their part to play in Lewis's apologetics. Such an 'imaginative apologetics' allows us to affirm the reasonableness of faith, while at the same time displaying its power to captivate the imagination. Christian churches need to ensure that their preaching, witness and worship express this rich vision of reality and lead others to wonder how they can go 'further up and further in' to the landscape of faith.

The Imagination and Apologetics

In 1946, Lewis was awarded the first of five honorary degrees – a doctorate of divinity from the University of St Andrews in Scotland. Professor Donald M. Baillie, speaking at the award ceremony on behalf of the university's Faculty of Divinity, explained the reason for their decision to honour Lewis in this way. Lewis, he declared, had 'succeeded in capturing the attention of many who will not readily listen to professional theologians', and had 'arranged a new kind of marriage between theological reflection and poetic imagination'.[17]

Baillie was accurate in his assessment of Lewis's significance. We've noted how Lewis had secured a huge readership for his popular religious writings. But what did Baillie mean by 'a new kind of marriage between theological reflection and poetic imagination'? And what is its relevance to apologetics?

We've already seen how Lewis's Chronicles of Narnia make an appeal to the imagination. In an earlier meeting, we looked at the way in which Lewis subverted Sigmund Freud's argument that God was merely a wish-fulfilment (see page 67). Lewis's tale of the sun and the lamp is not so much a logical argument as a new way of seeing things. Lewis gives us a way of realising that the argument that the sun is just an imaginary bigger and better lamp sounds clever – but is just plain wrong. So what of the related argument that Aslan is just an imaginary bigger and better cat? Or that God is just an imaginary bigger and better father? Lewis leaves us to work this out for ourselves. But it's not hard to work out where his approach takes us.

To reiterate a point we touched on earlier, Lewis sees reason and imagination as existing in a collaborative, not competitive, relationship. That's one of the reasons why Lewis uses analogies so much in his apologetics. Lewis wants us to see how some observation or experience fits within a Christian way of looking at things. It is like trying on a hat or shirt for size and looking at ourselves in a mirror. How well does it fit? How many of our observations of the world can a theory accommodate, and how persuasively? It is basically about seeing how our experiences of desire fit a Christian framework.

Take Lewis's 'argument from desire'. He basically argues that we experience desires that nothing in this world seems able to satisfy. And when we see these experiences through the lens of the Christian faith, we realise that this sort of experience is exactly what we would expect if Christianity were true. Christianity tells us that this is not our true home and that we were created for heaven. For Lewis, Christianity provides a clear way of seeing our desires: 'If I find in myself a desire which no experience in this world can satisfy, the most probable explanation is that I was made for another world.' Lewis invites his audience to see their experiences through a set of Christian spectacles and notice how these bring what might otherwise seem to be fuzzy or blurred into sharp focus.

Or consider his 'argument from morality'. This is sometimes portrayed in ridiculously simplistic terms – for example, 'experiencing a sense of moral obligation proves there is a God'. Lewis did not say this, and did not think this. As with the 'argument from desire', his argument is rather that the common human experience of a sense of moral obligation is easily and naturally accommodated within a Christian framework. The Christian lens brings things into focus. It enlightens the landscape of reality, allowing us to see how God, desire and morality are all held together within a greater scheme of things.

Lewis helps us to appreciate that apologetics need not take the form of deductive argument. Instead, apologetics can be an invitation to step into the Christian way of seeing things and explore how things look when seen from its standpoint. Lewis's approach says, 'Try seeing things this way!' If worldviews or metanarratives can be compared to lenses, which of them brings things into sharpest focus? This is not an irrational retreat from reason. Rather, it is about grasping a deeper order of things which is more easily accessed by the imagination than by reason. Yet once seen, its intrinsic rationality can be appreciated.

Again, Lewis's *explicit* appeal to reason involves an *implicit* appeal to the imagination. This may explain why Lewis's approach is still so fresh and popular despite its age. It appeals to both modern and postmodern outlooks. Lewis's imaginative reasoning bridges the chasm between modernity and postmodernity, insisting that both reason and imagination have their argumentative strengths because they are both part of a greater whole.

It's time to end this tutorial. But Lewis might well have one final word of advice to give us before we go our separate ways. A theme that often emerges in Lewis's writings of the late 1940s is that apologetics is exhausting and draining. Lewis makes this point explicitly in his 1945 lecture 'Christian Apologetics', in which he remarks that 'nothing is more dangerous to one's own faith than the work of an apologist'. Why? Not because there is anything irrational or incoherent about the Christian faith. It is, Lewis explains, the act of defending a doctrine that makes it seem 'spectral' or even 'unreal'.[18] Perhaps this helps us understand why Lewis later focused on works that explored the riches of faith – such as *The Four Loves* (1960). Lewis would remind us that apologists need to be looked after. They get spiritually drained.

This gives us an idea for what we might talk about next. Lewis established his reputation as an apologist with *The Problem of Pain*. So what can we learn from his approach to human suffering? We'll find out later. But there's another theme that we need to look at first. Lewis was a professional educationalist, who realised the importance of a deep immersion in knowledge for both culture and faith. So let's imagine that we're going to have lunch with Lewis, perhaps at The Eagle and Child in Oxford. What would he have to say about the importance of education?

6

A Love of Learning:
C.S. Lewis on Education

*For every one pupil who needs to be guarded from
a weak excess of sensibility there are three who need
to be awakened from the slumber of cold vulgarity.
The task of the modern educator is not to cut down
jungles but to irrigate deserts.*

C.S. Lewis, *The Abolition of Man*

One of Lewis's most trenchant books is *The Abolition of Man*, written in the depths of the Second
World War. This work seethes with anger. A barely
controlled rage permeates its pages. The subject which
provokes Lewis's extended anger is reflected in the
book's somewhat dull subtitle: 'Reflections on Education with Special Reference to the Teaching of English
in the Upper Forms of Schools'.

Why is education such a troubling subject? Why did
Lewis get so angry in such a dull book, which might
well have won a prize for having the most boring title
ever invented? Lewis would tell us that the answer is

simple: what we believe (or what we are taught to believe) has a massive impact on our values and actions. Lewis felt very strongly about this. He might have hammered our lunch table with his fists in frustration about approaches to education that were designed to suppress our deepest instincts about right and wrong, and open the way to an insipid moral relativism.

In *The Abolition of Man*, Lewis sets out to ridicule approaches to education that he believes are designed to produce 'men without chests' – people without any grounding in reality, unable to embrace good on the one hand and identify and reject evil on the other. How could someone resist the evil of Nazism without a firm grasp of what is right and what is wrong?

If we were facing a world war and Nazism, as Lewis was, our first instinct probably would not be to discuss the purpose of education, as Lewis did. Yet Lewis had understood the supreme importance of education in shaping our lives and values. 'What's the purpose of education?' isn't a question asked by idle people, safely ensconced in ivory towers, as we might suppose. Lewis insists it's a question on which our lives – and functioning societies – rest.

The Abolition of Man was prophetic, and is still reso-nant today. Lewis rejects the idea that education serves only 'instrumentalist' purposes – that education is simply about teaching students certain skills. He also exposes the inadequacy of superficial approaches to education which reject objective moral values. Lewis ridicules those who debunk traditional values and instead uncritically adopt whatever values happen to be fashionable at the time. 'Their scepticism about values is on the surface: it is for use on other people's values; about the values current in their own set they are not nearly sceptical enough.'[1] And this superficial approach neglects the wisdom of the past by focusing on the passing whims of the present – which are mistakenly assumed to be definitive and permanent. Lewis concludes that while people long for leaders who are virtuous and trustworthy, modern education under-mines these qualities by affirming moral relativism. We 'clamour for those very qualities we are rendering impossible'.[2]

So if these views are wrong, what is education all about? We might be tempted to ignore Lewis's strong opinions and dismiss the topic of education altogether, considering it the province of professionals. But Lewis insists that we realise the urgency of this question because how we view education has long-lasting effects, not just on our distinctly educational contexts – like our own schooling or that of our children – but on our outlook in life. It's the difference between utility and virtue. Many policy-makers now think of education in functional terms. It's about learning skills that will help students find employment – such as using a word pro-cessor or spreadsheet. Yet what about helping people to figure out the meaning of life? Or become good people? Or make a difference to others? Is education for a stage in life, completed once we find jobs, or should it be a lifelong pursuit?

Lewis stands for an older, more classical approach to education, which has been ignored rather than refuted. This vision of education aims to help people to love the good and hate the bad. Its aim is to help people become good and wise in all spheres of life, not simply to acquire knowledge or skills. Lewis is a prophetic voice in the face of fashionable educational trends, and we need to listen to him carefully.

But rather than get involved in a detailed discussion about *The Abolition of Man*, let's try to grasp Lewis's vision for education and see what we can learn from it. So let's imagine we are having lunch with Lewis. He steers the conversation towards the purpose and value of education. Where should we start? Perhaps the most obvious icebreaker is to ask Lewis to tell us how he himself came to be part of the world of education.

Lewis's Educational Career

Lewis's academic career was linked with England's greatest and oldest universities – Oxford and Cambridge. We don't know why Lewis decided to apply to study classics at Oxford University in 1916. What we do know is that he was absolutely convinced of the importance of learning and that this conviction ripened and deepened throughout his life. Although we mainly think of Lewis as an author, we need to remember that his professional calling was to teach English literature at Oxford and Cambridge.

Like most universities established during the Middle Ages, Oxford and Cambridge were 'collegiate'. They consisted of federations of autonomous colleges, with a central university administration. Students and academics at Oxford were invariably linked with a specific college, which was their main base of operations. Oxford colleges were not 'halls of residence', but independent societies of fellows and students. Lewis was linked with three colleges during his lifetime: University College, Oxford; Magdalen College, Oxford; and Magdalene College, Cambridge.

Lewis's academic career began at University College, Oxford, where he studied the philosophy, languages and history of the classical world. He then took a second undergraduate degree in English language and literature, cramming a three-year programme into a single year. It was obvious that Lewis was an outstanding student. By 1923, he had achieved the remarkable distinction of a 'triple first' – that is, gaining first-class honours at every stage of the assessment process. Lewis initially hoped to be a philosopher. His obvious talents led to his being employed as a tutor in philosophy at University College while the philosophy fellow spent a sabbatical year in the United States. Yet Lewis ended up a scholar of literature. In 1925, he was appointed as the tutorial fellow in English at Magdalen College, Oxford, one of the university's oldest, wealthiest and most prestigious colleges.

Lewis developed a specialist interest in the literature of the Middle Ages and Renaissance. His first major book established him as a commanding presence in the field. *The Allegory of Love* (1936) was recognised as outstanding by his academic colleagues, and the British Academy awarded Lewis the prestigious Sir Israel Gollancz Prize in 1937. Other scholarly works flowed from his pen.

Pen? Yes. Lewis never used a typewriter. He was born with a problem with his thumb joints, which made it difficult to type. All of Lewis's books were written by hand, even if someone else typed them up later. Lewis used the 'dip-pen' method. He would dip his fountain pen in a bottle of Quink ink, and then keep writing until the ink ran out – usually after about ten words.

But there was another reason for using this old-fashioned way of writing. Lewis felt that the 'clacking' of a typewriter would interfere with his sense of rhythm. He wanted to know what a text would sound like when read aloud. Lewis's emphasis on how texts sounded helps explain his success as a lecturer and broadcaster.

Many believe that Lewis's gifts as a teacher were seen at their best in his Oxford lectures and tutorials. Lewis rapidly gained a reputation as one of Oxford University's finest lecturers. Why? Three factors contributed to his remarkable success. First, Lewis was a good speaker. His rich, resonant voice – which one of his students described as a 'port wine and plum pudding voice' – was easy to listen to. While Lewis scored highly on this point, some of his Oxford colleagues were much less fortunate. J.R.R. Tolkien had a weak voice, which his audiences found uninteresting. Happily, Tolkien proved to be a more effective writer than he was a speaker!

Second, Lewis usually spoke without notes. Where he did use notes, these were minimal – for example, a brief list of quotes to be used, or points to be made. Lewis had a remarkable ability to remember texts – including both literary classics and his own lecture notes. Lewis's critic William Empson remarked that Lewis 'was the best read man of his generation, one who read everything and remembered everything he read'.[3] Lewis committed his lectures to memory and was able to dispense with notes. Unlike many Oxford academics, who merely read their lecture scripts aloud, Lewis believed that good communication demanded that he engage with his audiences. In a 1924 letter to his father, Lewis remarked that lectures that were simply read out to their audiences tended to 'send people to sleep'.[4] He realised that he would have to learn to talk to his audiences, not simply recite his lectures to them. His students loved his lecturing style, which contrasted sharply with that of other members of Oxford's Faculty of English.

Third, Lewis's lectures were marked by more than their superb delivery. Their content was widely agreed to be remarkable. Lewis seemed to have an ability to grasp and communicate the internal structure of leading works of literature – above all, John Milton's classic *Paradise Lost*. Somehow Lewis seemed able to avoid bombarding his students with facts and instead helped them to see the 'big picture' offered by writers such as Milton or Edmund Spenser. Where others fussed about points of textual detail, Lewis opened up the great themes that lay behind the writers' works.

Lewis also served as Magdalen College's tutor in English. At that point, the heart of Oxford University's educational method lay in the tutorial system. Each week, undergraduates at Magdalen College studying English would meet with Lewis for an hour. During this time, they would read aloud an essay, which would then be discussed and debated. Lewis's students at Oxford found themselves forced to defend and develop their ideas. They were not allowed to get away with sweeping generalisations or simplistic assertions. Lewis would stop them and ask them to explain exactly what they meant. And once they explained it, they had to defend it.

Lewis found himself increasingly caught up in the world of academic politics in Oxford, especially within the Faculty of English. Should the curriculum be extended to include more recent writings? Lewis found himself on the wrong side of many of these debates with his colleagues and became increasingly unhappy at Oxford. Happily, a development at Oxford's great intellectual rival provided a way out of this situation. In 1954, Lewis was appointed as the first holder of a new professorship in Medieval and Renaissance English. His move to Cambridge was remarkably successful and seems to have led to a new lease on life. Recognition of his outstanding talent followed. In July 1955, Lewis was elected a Fellow of the British Academy, the greatest honour a British academic can hope to achieve.

Lewis, then, was widely regarded as an outstanding academic. But what did he think about the process of education itself? How should it be done? What was it for? What might Lewis want to highlight in our conversation? Let's focus in on a few themes that Lewis considered to be of major importance.

Chronological Snobbery: Why the Latest Isn't Always the Best

In our second conversation with Lewis, we noted a quote from Francis Bacon: 'Old wood best to burn, old wine to drink, old friends to trust, and old authors to read.' The mature Lewis would have enjoyed this, nodding his head in agreement, especially at the final five words. Yet the young Lewis had little sympathy for the ideas of old authors. He lived in a bright new world. Why mess it up with the failed ideas of the past? An old author was an outdated author, perhaps a relic to be studied but not an adviser to be heeded.

During the 1920s, Lewis became friends with Owen Barfield, an undergraduate at Wadham College. The two young men debated many issues, sometimes playfully, sometimes with frightening intensity. At that time, Lewis had adopted what he called his 'New Look' – a way of thinking that was dismissive of the ideas and values of the past.

Lewis might well have agreed with the industrialist Henry Ford, who famously declared that 'history is bunk'.[5] The present has enough problems without worrying about the past. Who wants to be held back by the past when the world is changing so quickly? The past is a liability, not a resource. At best, it's a waste of time. At worst, it locks us into an outmoded way of thinking. Why not ignore it altogether?

Lewis thought like that in the early 1920s. There was a tension here with Lewis's interests in the classic world of ancient Greece and Rome. He seems to have thought that you studied Plato and Aristotle mainly to appreciate how much we've moved on since then. Like the New Testament, these writers were locked into a bygone age and had little relevance to the brave new world that was opening up in the aftermath of the greatest and most destructive war in the history of humanity.

Yet Barfield persuaded Lewis that he was simply wrong in being so dismissive of the past. Lewis came to see that he had fallen into the trap of 'chronological snobbery' – that is, an 'uncritical acceptance of the intellectual climate common to our own age and the assumption that whatever has gone out of date is on that account discredited'.[6] Lewis came to see that the reading of literature – especially *older* literature – is an important challenge to this kind of 'chronological snobbery'. The most recent is not necessarily the best. It is still on trial and has yet to be assessed properly.

Lewis's essay 'On the Reading of Old Books' (1944) is especially forceful on this point. He argues that knowledge of the literature of the past provides readers with a seasoned viewpoint, allowing them to see 'the controversies of the moment in their proper perspective'.[7] Reading old books, Lewis continues, helps us avoid becoming captives of the 'Spirit of the Age' by keeping 'the clean sea breeze of the centuries blowing through our minds'.[8]

For Lewis, people are too easily taken in by the latest cultural and intellectual fashions. Wanting to be 'up to date' in their thinking, they uncritically accept the latest ideas they read about in the media. Reading older books, Lewis argues, helps us to realise that 'basic assumptions have been quite different in different periods'. We need to remember that the ideas we tend to regard as hopelessly old fashioned and out of date were once seen as cutting edge. What was once new and brilliant becomes old and stale. Perhaps Lewis seems a little too scathing when he declares that 'much which seems certain to the uneducated is merely temporary fashion'.[9] Yet his point is fair: much recent thought is fleeting, lacking the staying power to excite and inform later generations.

So is Lewis saying that only old ideas are any good and that new ideas are invariably wrong? No.[10] He is asking us to be *critical*. New ideas need to be looked at carefully. They may be good; they may be bad. But ideas are not *automatically* good because they are new. Similarly, many – but not all – old ideas have permanent value. They have proved themselves through the centuries and will continue to be important in the future. We need to figure out which ideas and values are of lasting importance, and hold fast to them.

Let's look at an example to help us understand what Lewis has in mind. Lewis became an Oxford don in the mid-1920s. At this time, the British cultural elite were enthralled by eugenics. Eugenics was the brainchild of Charles Darwin's cousin Francis Galton and was developed in response to Darwin's theory of natural selection. Rather than leave the future of the human race to chance, advocates of eugenics aimed to replace natural selection with a planned and deliberate selection. Genetic planning was seen as a no-brainer, as natural and important to future societies as town planning.[11]

Eugenics was seen as progressive and scientific, the natural outcome of Darwinism. To ensure the future of the human race, it was argued, certain types of people ought to be prevented from breeding. They would pollute the gene pool. The leading lights of the secular left lined up to support this bright new idea. It rapidly became the politically correct thing to think for British Socialists of the 1920s and 1930s.

H.G. Wells was convinced that humankind would drift to extinction unless the cultural elite took control of the evolutionary process. Wells believed that Lenin's revolution in Russia represented an important step in that direction. He arranged to meet Lenin in 1920 and found him to be 'a good type of scientific man'. Wells was aware that the new Soviet Union seemed to be killing rather large numbers of people. But Wells believed this was the price of fashioning a new humanity. To secure the future, you had to eliminate undesirables.[12] The rest of the world had a lot to learn from Lenin, he told his trusting readers. And some of them believed him.

Membership in the Eugenics Society peaked during the 1930s. George Bernard Shaw declared that 'the selective breeding of man' was essential for the future of society. H. G. Wells was even more emphatic and enthusiastic. Eugenics would lead to the removal 'of detrimental types and characteristics' and the 'fostering of desirable types' in their place. It was only when Adolf Hitler championed eugenics that Western progressive thinkers began to realise that something had gone terribly wrong. But by then, it was too late.

Lewis was one of the most effective critics of H. G. Wells in the 1930s and 1940s. His three science-fiction novels each represent critiques of Wells's approach. For Lewis, eugenics was simply inhuman. The movement might seem to be bright and progressive, given credibility by being grounded in science. Yet the way it was promoted was an example of 'chronological snobbery'. It was assumed that its scientific credentials and novelty were enough to justify it. Today, almost nobody takes it seriously. It is widely regarded as repressive. Yet it was openly advocated by the secular left in the 1930s as one of the best hopes for the future of the human race. Lewis's words of caution clearly need to be taken seriously. New ideas can be supremely *bad* ideas – and by the time people realise just how bad they are, it's sometimes difficult to get rid of them.

But there's another point that Lewis wants to make. When we read an older book – say, a treatise on science dating from the sixteenth century – we often feel patronising about its ideas. 'That's what they thought back then! But who would think that today? We've moved on.' Our own ideas, we believe, are so much better.

Lewis asks us to realise that we have fallen into a trap. We're assuming that our own ideas are right. What we need to appreciate is that *every* age assumes its ideas are right. Lewis suggests that we imagine how future readers – say, a century from now – will look back at some of the settled assumptions of our age. They might well think about our ideas what we think about older ideas today.

Do you see what Lewis is doing? He is using our critical attitude towards the past to *anticipate* the judgement that the future will make about us! We can't just assume that the most recent is the best. We need to realise that posterity will discard much of what we value, but will retain some of it as having permanent value. What Lewis wants us to do is to identify what is junk and what is valuable.

Yet Lewis does more than call into question the idea that the most recent is the best. He challenges the idea that we ourselves know best. It's one of the most natural assumptions that we can make: 'This is how we see it – and this is how it is.' Lewis invites us to see things through other eyes and expand our vision of reality as a result.

Let's get Lewis to develop this point. What does he mean by expanding our vision?

An Expansion of Our Vision

Lewis thinks of education as an 'enlargement of our vision' or an 'expansion of our minds'. The basic idea is found in many classical writers, who see education as a way of rescuing us from our own limitations. We know how we ourselves see things. But is this the best way? And how do we discover alternatives?

Lewis offers a brilliant answer, which maintains our individuality while at the same time opening us up to deeper and richer ways of seeing things. Literature offers us a different way of seeing things. The reading of literature opens our eyes, offering us new perspectives on things that we can evaluate and adopt.

> My own eyes are not enough for me, I will see through those of others . . . In reading great literature, I become a thousand men and yet remain myself. Like the night sky in the Greek poem, I see with a myriad eyes, but it is still I who see.[13]

Reading literature, Lewis suggests, enables us 'to see with other eyes, to imagine with other imaginations, to feel with other hearts, as well as our own'.[14]

Reading works of literature is about 'entering fully into the opinions, and therefore also the attitudes, feelings, and total experience' of other people.[15] To read literature is thus to open us up to new ideas, or to force us to revisit those we once believed we were right to reject.

Lewis isn't necessarily asking us to give up on our own ideas. In many ways, he is inviting us to go further and deeper. Sometimes we are right to reject ideas. But we need to be able to understand why we do so. After all, we may well encounter someone who holds those ideas. Our engagement will be much more satisfactory and positive if we understand where those ideas come from and have thought through responses to them.

Yet at other times, reading literature helps us to realise we have failed to appreciate the power of certain ideas, or their ability to make sense of things. For Lewis, learning at its best is about 'trying on' ways of looking at the world and seeing how well they work. Lewis's own conversion to Christianity took place partly for this reason. When reading Christian literature, Lewis came to realise that there was something special, something realistic and true, about its representation of things that contrasted favourably with secular alternatives. Lewis came to see reading Christian literature as one of the things that brought him back to faith: 'A young man who wishes to remain a sound Atheist cannot be too careful of his reading. There are traps everywhere.'[16]

As Lewis makes clear in *Surprised by Joy*, Christian writers such as George Herbert and John Donne helped him realise that their way of seeing things worked remarkably well. Might this, he wondered, be because they were *right*? It was an uncomfortable thought for Lewis, who at that time was still clinging to his increasingly fragile atheist faith.

Yet for Lewis, education is about more than being familiar with other ways of thinking or looking at things. It is about *inhabiting* them – in other words, *experiencing* the way of thinking and living that they make possible. Lewis uses a nice analogy to help us understand the point he is making – English tourists, so vividly and amusingly portrayed in E.M. Forster's novel *A Room with a View* (1908). Some tourists, Lewis argues, visit foreign countries without any intention of being challenged by them. They bring their own tea with them so that they don't have to drink the local alternative. They keep themselves at a distance from the local culture and see their 'Englishness' as something to be preserved at all costs.[17] And when they return home, they are untainted by their experience.

For Lewis, *real* tourists are those who are prepared to learn from their experience abroad. They eat the local food and drink the local wine, seeing 'the foreign country as it looks, not to the tourist, but to its inhabitants'. As a result, Lewis argues, these English tourists come home 'modified, thinking and feeling' in different ways. Their travel has enlarged their vision of things.

Education is about *changing* us – helping us realise that we are not always right and that we can gain a deeper and better grasp of reality by experiencing the world the way others do. Although Lewis sees this as characteristic of good education as a whole, he also sees it as being important for the education of Christians, who need to go deeper and further into their faith. Let's look at what he has in mind.

Going Deeper: Lewis on Learning and the Christian Life

Oxford dons can be cruel to one another. I love the way a college academic dismissed one of his colleagues: 'On the surface, he's profound, but deep down, he's superficial.' One of the major themes of Lewis's approach to education is the need to go deeper and to enlarge our vision of reality. This general approach has particular relevance to Christianity. As I read Lewis in my early twenties, I realised how shallow my faith was. Something would have to be done about that. And, as it turned out, I found Lewis enormously helpful in deepening my grasp of my faith.

So how does Lewis apply his ideas about education to his own faith? How can learning help us in the Christian life? Let's pick up on a phrase that Lewis coined in a letter of February 1952: 'Deep Church'.[18] Lewis used this phrase to mean an attitude of valuing and an act of reconnecting with the Christian tradition. Unlike liberalism and modernism, which Lewis regarded as late and unwelcome arrivals on the Christian scene, a basic consensual Christian orthodoxy has always existed and still has the potential to enrich – without stifling – church life today. Lewis's severe criticisms of the intellectual pretensions of secular modernity and the spiritual emptiness of the 'Christianity-and-water' religion of professed liberals rested on his conviction that both were betrayals of something far more important and worthwhile – namely, 'Deep Church'.

For Lewis, Christianity is at its best when it is rooted in the past and engaged with the present. In explaining what he meant by 'Deep Church', Lewis declared that it designated 'the Christian religion as understood *ubique et ab omnibus*' – a shortened form of a Latin tagline meaning 'the faith believed everywhere and by everyone' – in other words, a basic consensual orthodoxy. Lewis put it like this in 1944: we need a 'standard of plain, central Christianity ("mere Christianity" as Baxter called it)'.[19] This is not some 'insipid' minimalist conception of Christianity, reduced to its lowest common denominator. Rather, it is 'something positive, self-consistent, and inexhaustible'. It is like a 'great level viaduct', channelling the life-giving water of faith down the ages towards us, so that it might refresh and resource us.

Lewis invites us to think of the Church's history as a long conversation about how best to interpret the Bible and to express and appreciate the rich ideas it contains. We need to connect with that conversation from its beginnings if we are to understand its later forms. 'If you join at eleven o'clock a conversation which began at eight you will often not see the real bearing of what is said.'[20]

So how are we to do this? Whom should we be reading? Lewis mentions a series of writers that he personally found helpful – such as the poets George Herbert and Thomas Traherne, and the theologians Augustine of Hippo and Thomas Aquinas.[21] But these are not necessarily the writers that *we* should read. Lewis's choices clearly reflect his personal interests (remember, he was a professional student of English literature). Who else might be helpful?

One obvious example for us is Lewis himself. One of the reasons why Lewis's *Mere Christianity* has been so successful is that it represents a distillation of the kind of 'deep' Christianity that Lewis both admired and expressed. *Mere Christianity* could be said to capture the clean and refreshing 'sea breeze of the centuries' in a bottle, so that we can benefit from Lewis's labours of reading without having to repeat them ourselves. Lewis's Christian mind was shaped mainly by the solid classical heritage of Plato, Athanasius of Alexandria, Augustine of Hippo, Thomas Aquinas, Thomas à Kempis, George Herbert and Thomas Traherne, given added imaginative and apologetic spice from George MacDonald and G.K. Chesterton.

To read Lewis is to connect with the 'great tradition' of Christian thought, expressed in a winsome and palatable way. Lewis is like a gateway, making the riches of 'Deep Church' more accessible. In my own case, I found that reading some of Lewis's more substantial works – such as his 1941 sermon 'The Weight of Glory' – made me want to read writers such as Augustine of Hippo and Dante, while at the same time preparing me for some of their ideas and approaches. I don't want to demean Lewis in any way by this comparison, but he was like a tour guide, quickly pointing out notable landmarks and giving me thumbnail sketches of their significance. Lewis made me want to visit these landmarks on my own, and find out more. And when I visited them, I found that they both confirmed and exceeded what I found in Lewis's introductions.

But there are others – writers who stand within the 'great tradition' of the Christian faith – who can enrich our own grasp of our faith and make us better Christians. As someone who specialises in the history of Christian thought, I have noticed that some of the best recent books draw on older writers, putting their wisdom and insight at the service of a new generation. As so many have found, the antidote to a stale faith can lie in drinking deeply from these refreshing and life-giving springs – including Lewis himself.

So what is the purpose of education? Lewis would point to the way that it breaks our focus on the present, enlarges our view of the world and encourages us to explore the depths of our faith. All of these together, while not guaranteed to make us discover and love the good and dismiss the bad, will help us as we seek to live godly lives. And they will also help us to hold on to the good in times of trouble, the subject of our next conversation with Lewis.

7

Coping with Suffering:
C.S. Lewis on the Problem of Pain

Can a mortal ask questions which God finds unan-
swerable? Quite easily, I should think. All nonsense
questions are unanswerable. How many hours are
there in a mile? Is yellow square or round? Probably
half the questions we ask – half our great theologi-
cal and metaphysical problems – are like that.

C.S. Lewis, *A Grief Observed*

One of the most attractive and winsome themes in Lewis's thought is his insistence that Christianity offers an imaginatively rich and rationally satisfying 'big picture' of life. It makes sense of what we observe around us and experience within us. Lewis took particular pleasure in comparing the Christian faith to a rising sun: just as the sun illuminates the landscape, allowing us to see things that were otherwise hidden in darkness, so God casts light on a dark world.

But is it quite that simple? Now that we've had so many conversations with Lewis, we might feel a little more confident challenging him! Does his sun analogy mean that everything is clearly seen? Does it mean that all the shadows vanish as the sun rises? Certainly not! What about the existence of suffering and pain in the world? Surely that raises some difficult questions.

And Lewis would agree. Christianity brings things into sharper focus than any other worldview does, but that doesn't mean everything comes into sharp focus. It doesn't mean everything is brightly illuminated. The shadowlands are still there – patches of darkness that the rising sun never fully illuminates. And that means there will be times when the journey of faith leads us through the shadows and into darkness. We encounter things that we do not understand and cannot control. For most Christians, the area of our faith that causes intellectual and emotional discomfort is suffering. Surely there is something wrong here. Why does a good God allow it? And what does suffering mean for our lives?

It's easy to dismiss Lewis as an 'ivory tower' thinker, detached from the harshness of real life. The reality, however, is that Lewis knew suffering first hand, and spent much time reflecting about it. Two of his books – *The Problem of Pain* and *A Grief Observed* – are devoted to this issue. He clearly thought it important. So let's imagine that we're having a cup of tea with Lewis in his rooms at Magdalen College. As the kettle boils, we might begin by asking him to tell his own story, and the role that suffering has played in it.

Lewis's Experiences of Suffering

Hollywood is great at telling stories; it's lousy at doing history. The movie *Shadowlands* tells the story – or at least its own version of the story – of Lewis's marriage to the American divorcée Joy Davidman and his response to the tragedy of her death from cancer. Everyone who knew Lewis was scathing about its portrayal of Lewis as a socially withdrawn and emotionally distant bachelor, whose life was turned upside down when he fell in love with the demure Joy Davidman.

Yet the most worrying thing about the movie is its core assumption that Lewis was naive, an Oxford don living a cosy and sheltered life which was rudely interrupted by his wife's cancer. The movie suggests that Davidman's illness and death showed Lewis that his simplistic faith couldn't cope with this complex reality and implies that he ended up adopting some form of rather insipid humanism.

This is simply nonsense. So let's begin by setting the record straight. For the first nine years of his life, Lewis enjoyed a sheltered life. Albert Lewis, his wife Flora and their two sons enjoyed a comfortable lifestyle in middle-class Belfast. Albert Lewis's legal practice was doing well and generated enough income to allow them to move into a large new house in the prosperous Strandtown area of the city. But in 1908, Lewis's world fell to pieces. His mother was diagnosed with cancer. She died, slowly and painfully, at home in August 1908.

It was a devastating experience for Lewis. We find him hinting at its lingering pain in *The Magician's Nephew*. Digory Kirke's mother is lovingly described on her deathbed, in terms that seem to echo Lewis's haunting memories of the final days of his own mother's life: 'There she lay, as he had seen her like so many other times, propped up on the pillows, with a thin, pale face that would make you cry to look at.'[1]

Like many of his generation, Lewis was exposed to the massive trauma of the Great War. While serving in the trenches of north-western France, Lewis had witnessed sickening scenes of death, destruction and suffering – such as 'horribly smashed men' and 'sitting or standing corpses'.[2] Who could believe in God in the face of such devastation?

Lewis composed some of his early cycle of poems for *Spirits in Bondage* around this time. His 'Ode for New Year's Day' was written when under fire from German artillery near the French town of Arras in January 1918. This poem solemnly declares the final death of a God who was in any case a human invention. Any idea that the 'red God' might 'lend an ear' to human cries of misery lay discredited and abandoned in the mud, a disgraced 'Power who slays'. Lewis himself became a victim of the war. He was wounded in battle in April 1918. Shortly afterwards, while recovering in hospital, Lewis learned that his best friend, Paddy Moore, had been killed in battle.

When Lewis returned to Oxford in January 1919 to resume his studies, he was a battle-hardened atheist. His body was permanently scarred from shrapnel wounds. Still deeper, however, were the wounds inflicted on his soul. Lewis was cynical about religion and dismissive of belief in God. He had experienced more trauma than most of his modern readers ever will.

Yet Lewis's atheism began to falter, eventually to crumble. By 1930, Lewis had experienced a 'reconversion'; by the summer of 1932, he had grasped the full imaginative and rational power of Christianity. As *The Pilgrim's Regress* (1933) makes clear, Lewis now saw life in a very different way.

So how did Lewis's new way of seeing things affect the way in which he understood pain and suffering? There are three major points at which Lewis deals with suffering. The first is the book which brought him to attention as an apologist – *The Problem of Pain* (1940). The second is the final novel in the Chronicles of Narnia, *The Last Battle* (1956). In it Lewis offers a way of seeing the sufferings of this present age in the light of the coming of the new Narnia. The third, of course, is the emotionally raw engagement with suffering in *A Grief Observed* (1961). We'll consider both *The Problem of Pain* and *A Grief Observed* in this discussion.

So let's imagine that we are comfortably seated in the shabby old armchairs in Lewis's room in Magdalen College. As we settle down, we might ask Lewis to tell us about his first major attempt to engage suffering. What ideas did he explore in *The Problem of Pain*, and what method did he use? By now, the kettle has boiled and Lewis is making a steaming pot of tea, as he prepares to tell us his thoughts on pain.

The Problem of Pain

As we learned in an earlier meeting, Lewis was invited to write *The Problem of Pain* in 1939 by Ashley Sampson, the owner of a small London publishing imprint. He wondered if Lewis might contribute a volume to a series of books he had edited, dealing with challenges to Christianity. Would Lewis write a volume on the problem of pain? Lewis agreed. It was his first work of apologetics.

So what approach did he take? As the movie *Shadowlands* indicates, Lewis's approach to suffering in *The Problem of Pain* is often summarised in a single citation. Suffering is God's 'megaphone to rouse a deaf world'.[3] This is a rather shallow and simplistic summary of both that book and Lewis's position in general. At one point, Lewis reflected on the way in which suffering can help us to become better people. One small part of that small section of *The Problem of Pain* could be summed up in that citation. However, the full quotation perhaps makes Lewis's meaning clearer: 'God whispers to us in our pleasures, speaks in our conscience, but shouts in our pains: it is His megaphone to rouse a deaf world.'[4]

Lewis makes it clear from the outset that *The Problem of Pain* will not deal with the place of pain in the Christian life. He does not consider himself sufficiently qualified to speak of the way in which pain can help us learn 'fortitude and patience'. His goal is rather to 'solve the intellectual problem' that is raised by suffering.[5] This focus leads Lewis to treat pain in an overintellectualised way, which has bewildered some of his readers. Surely Lewis knew that suffering was more than some kind of intellectual crossword puzzle?

Yet we must allow Lewis to deal with the issue on his own terms. Remember, he had been asked to contribute a volume to a series which focused on intellectual aspects of the Christian faith. In accepting the invitation, he had to respect the editor's briefing about the approach he was to take. Furthermore, it is clear that Lewis treats the 'problem' of pain as lying not so much in its emotional impact as in its suggestion that reality is fundamentally irrational. If the world does not make sense, then it is meaningless.

Lewis opens the book by reminding – or perhaps informing – his readers that he used to be an atheist himself. There are hints everywhere in this opening chapter of the themes raised, but not answered, in *Spirits in Bondage* – human suffering in the face of a seemingly deaf heaven and a silent God. Lewis sketches the universe he himself once believed in, a futile place of darkness and cold, of misery and suffering. This is a universe bound to die, a world in which civilisations pointlessly rise and die, and a human race that science condemns to a final extinction.

In the face of all this pointlessness, Lewis explains to his readers that he initially concluded, 'Either there is no spirit behind the universe, or else a spirit indifferent to good and evil, or else an evil spirit.'[6] Yet doubts began to arise in his mind. Is it really that straightforward? 'If the universe is so bad, or even half so bad, how on earth did human beings ever come to attribute it to the activity of a wise and good Creator?' Pain is only a 'problem' from a Christian perspective. If the universe is meaningless, no explanation need be offered. Pain is meaningless, like everything else.

One of Lewis's core points is that pain is the price that we pay for being alive. Life is a high-value item, and it comes at a cost. 'Try to exclude the possibility of suffering which the order of nature and the existence of free-wills involve, and you will find that you have excluded life itself.'[7] We need to get used to the existence of pain. That's just the way things are.

But there is a problem, Lewis suggests. He frames it like this: 'If God were good, He would make His creatures perfectly happy, and if He were almighty He would be able to do what He wished.'[8] The existence of pain calls this into question. Yet Lewis points out that we need to look more closely at the meaning of these words – such as 'good'. In the everyday sense of the words, there is a problem. But what if they have special meanings when used about God? For example, what if we confuse 'goodness' with 'kindness'? We would then approach the problem of pain from a false perspective.

Lewis suggests that this is indeed what has happened. We have failed to appreciate what the 'goodness' of God truly means, and have misunderstood it as an essentially sentimental idea. We must, Lewis declares, learn to see ourselves as the true objects of God's love – a love which has our best interests at heart, even though we are unable to see or implement these for ourselves. Suffering can show us when we take wrong turns or do bad things. It can bring home to us the frailty and transience of our existence and challenge our belief that we can get by on our own.

Pain thus helps to shatter the illusion that 'all is well', allowing God to plant 'the flag of truth within the fortress of a rebel soul'.[9] And it can help us make good choices. Since we, as sinners, tend to rebel against God, there has to be some means by which God can redirect us, helping us to see where we have gone wrong. We would prefer to be left alone, not loved as passionately as this.

Lewis's argument here is primarily logical, making little appeal to either the emotions or the imagination. We need to get our concept of goodness right, instead of being led astray by what we would now probably call a consumerist understanding of goodness – namely, something that makes us happy, or at least makes us feel better. Lewis asks us to trust that God loves us and wishes the best for us – and wisely sees things that we do not.

To help us grasp this difficult point, Lewis asks us to reflect on four different types of relationships and consider the role that pain plays within each of these.[10] Each of these analogies, or models, helps us understand some aspect of the loving relationship between the Creator and the creation. Unusually, each of these analogies is taken directly from the Bible. (Lewis tends to use analogies drawn from literature.)

Lewis's first analogy is the love of an artist for his creation. Lewis is here thinking of Jeremiah's description of the relationship of a potter to the clay (see Jeremiah 18). Whenever the potter sees a flaw in the vessel he is producing from a lump of clay, he will start again. The clay is flattened and the moulding process begins once more. The point that Lewis wants us to appreciate is that the potter has a vision for the clay and will not rest until that vision is complete. Remoulding is thus to be seen as a mark of commitment, even if this 'creation' is an inanimate object, such as a clay vessel or a building.

Lewis now makes a further point using this same analogy. Any artist is going to take trouble over anything he makes. But what if this is a really important project? What if an artist is trying to paint 'the picture of his life' – in other words, the work which marks the height of his career and for which he will be remembered? Wouldn't he take especial trouble over this? Wouldn't he want to get this one just right? Lewis then reminds us that human beings are the height of God's creation. And that means that God takes special trouble over us. He wants to get us right.

The second analogy is the 'love of a man for a beast'. Lewis has in mind here the relationship between people and their dogs. The Lewis family had pets in Belfast in the early 1900s, and a series of pet dogs lived at Lewis's home in Oxford. This is an analogy that he feels completely at home with. Puppies have to be trained. Why? So they are healthier and will live longer. The puppies, of course, are quite unaware of the benefits of the training they are receiving and probably see it as the irritating imposition of pain. If the puppy were a theologian, Lewis remarks, it would probably have a rather dark view of human goodness. But this training not only leads to a healthier life for the dog but also opens up a world beyond the natural ability of a dog – such as affection and comfort.

Lewis's third analogy is that of a father's love for his son. We must assume that at this point Lewis had in mind his own somewhat dysfunctional relationship with Albert Lewis. The father loves his son and wants to prepare him for the challenges he will face in the world. Just as important, he is aware that his son will not fully understand the 'risks and dangers' to which he will be exposed, and must therefore discipline him as a means of protecting him from these dangers.

Finally, Lewis turns to the relationship between a man and a woman, noting that the Bible often uses this model to illuminate God's relationship with his people. God's relationship with Israel is often compared to two lovers, just as God's relationship with the Church is often compared to a husband and wife. True love is about *perfecting* the beloved. Lewis's point here is that our relationships with people who really matter to us lead towards change and development on our part. True love involves a willingness to change, to become more like the ones we love. Love is dynamic, not static. God may accept us just as we are – but he isn't going to leave us there. God wants to move us on, to help us become the people we are meant to be.

Through these four analogies, Lewis sets out to show that real love is transformative. It is not a passive acquiescence in our present state, but a passionate commitment to enable us to transcend our limits and become better people. 'You asked for a loving God: you have one.'[11]

Yet there is at least one point at which Lewis moves away from the somewhat cold and clinical realm of logic and moves towards a more imaginative approach. Following his night-time conversation with J.R.R. Tolkien and Hugo Dyson in September 1931, Lewis had come to appreciate the power of the Christian story. In *The Problem of Pain*, Lewis supplements his essentially philosophical analysis of the problem of suffering by exploring the story of the death of Jesus Christ. Lewis had chosen as an epigraph George MacDonald's remark that 'the Son of God suffered unto death, not that men might not suffer, but that their sufferings might be like His'. The incarnation of God in Christ, for Lewis, must be the focus of a Christian answer to the problem of pain. 'God saw the crucifixion in the act of creating the first nebula.'[12] Suffering is something built into the structure of the universe. But it is also something that God saw as a means of perfecting his creation.

Now that's all very interesting. But does it really solve anything? It doesn't really help all that much to say that the suffering Christians experience in life is a bit like inflicting pain on a dog to make it behave in ways that will extend its lifespan and make it more useful. And while many readers find Lewis's *Problem of Pain* satisfying, others feel that it leaves too many questions unanswered and perhaps offers too logical a solution to a problem that is really emotional or existential.

Lewis seems to have realised that there were difficulties with his approach. Perhaps that is why some see the final chapter of the work as offering an important pointer towards a satisfying solution. In this chapter, titled 'Heaven',[13] Lewis explores how the Christian vision of heaven informs our experience of suffering. Although Lewis's focus here is primarily on human individuality, we find themes developed that will be explored more rigorously elsewhere – especially in the 1941 sermon 'The Weight of Glory'. One of these is of particular interest.

Puzzles and Mysteries

The Problem of Pain was written at the beginning of the Second World War. The same fear of German bombing of major southern British cities that led to the evacuation of children from London to places such as Oxford also led to the imposition of a 'blackout'. At night, cities such as Oxford were plunged into darkness so that they could not be seen from the air. All street lights were turned off; homes were fitted with blinds to prevent any light from escaping. As a result, cities at night were completely unlit.

We've already looked at how Lewis conceives 'understanding' as 'seeing'. Lewis used this analogy to suggest that the life of faith is like walking at night in a blackout.[14] We don't see everything clearly. There isn't enough light. But 'the blackout is not quite complete. There are chinks.' At times we glimpse the bigger picture, which reassures us that there is a hidden order and deeper structure. Pain and suffering may make the world appear to be irrational, yet every now and then, there is a chink in the blind and we can see further. We discover that 'an unattainable ecstasy' has hovered just beyond our reach, creating a longing for a better world, which is heightened still further by suffering and pain.

The point that Lewis wants us to appreciate is that the world may at times *seem* to be meaningless. But that is because we live in a darkened world and we cannot see with complete clarity. We are frail, and there are limits to our vision. One day, Lewis argues, things will become clear to us – including the place of suffering within creation. In the meantime, we must be patient and ask what we can learn from this. How can suffering help us become better people?

This is a much more promising approach. Lewis highlights that there are limits to our understanding. We just can't take everything in. Our minds are too small; the world is too dark. There are bound to be areas of mystery, like the far side of a mountain glacier, where the sun never manages to penetrate.

Let's make a distinction between a *puzzle* and a *mystery*. Austin Farrer, one of Lewis's closest friends at Oxford University, used this distinction a lot. It came naturally to him, as his wife was a noted author of crime fiction.[15] Farrer realised that most detective novels are really puzzles rather than mysteries. Once the reader has enough information, there is nothing to stop him or her from solving the puzzle and producing a nice, neat answer. As long as the information is pieced together properly, a good detective novel allows the reader to work out the identity of the murderer through cool and clinical logic. A puzzle is just a problem that we can solve when we can get hold of enough information.

But not all problems, Farrer argues, are puzzles. Some are *mysteries*, lying beyond the ability of the human mind to grasp. So what stops us from grasping mysteries properly? Why can't we solve them? Farrer insists that it is not a lack of information, but something more fundamental. Our minds simply are not big enough to take in these mysteries. There are no slick and neat solutions here. We catch glimpses of possible solutions, but they always seem to lie beyond our reach. Puzzles lead to logical answers; mysteries often force us to stretch language to its limits in an attempt to describe a reality that is just too great to take in properly.

It's easy to see how this distinction helps us think about suffering. It's not a puzzle; it's a mystery. It's not something we can dissect using cool logic. Farrer pushes us to realise that there are limits to our understanding. A failure to understand something does not mean it is irrational. It may simply mean that it lies on the far side of our limited abilities to take things in and make complete sense of them.

Now Farrer develops ideas that we find in Lewis. And it's a helpful distinction. Pain is not a puzzle we can solve, as if it were a crossword. It's a mystery that simply exceeds our ability to understand it.[16] And that helps a lot.

A Grief Observed

We noted earlier that the late 1940s was a time of considerable difficulty for Lewis. Mrs Moore, the mother of Paddy Moore, had lived with Lewis since 1919. In the late 1940s, she became increasingly disturbed psychologically. Lewis was unable to look after her at home. He became clinically exhausted and had to place her in a private nursing home. He visited her daily, and never let her know that he was worried he would not be able to afford to keep on paying the home's rather demanding fees. In the end, Mrs Moore died in an influenza epidemic that swept Britain in early 1951.

Yet the illness and death of Mrs Moore seems to have heightened Lewis's sense of the transitory nature of life. Pain and suffering did not simply call into question the rationality of the world. They were pointers to human mortality and frailty, a reminder that life does not go on for ever.

After the death of Mrs Moore in 1951, most of Lewis's close friends expected him to remain a bachelor for the rest of his life. Lewis had shown no romantic interest in any woman. Yet on Monday 23 April 1956, Lewis married Joy Davidman in a civil ceremony at Oxford's Register Office.[17] Davidman was an American divorcée who had befriended Lewis during visits to England in 1952 and 1953. Shortly after their marriage, things went tragically wrong. In October 1956, Davidman fell while trying to answer a telephone call. She was admitted to the hospital, where X-rays showed a broken femur. But they also showed a malignant tumour in her left breast, as well as secondary tumours elsewhere. Her days were numbered. She died at the age of forty-five in Oxford on 13 July 1960, with Lewis by her bedside.

Lewis was devastated. Davidman's death unleashed a stream of raw emotion and doubt. In the end, Lewis wrote these doubts and emotions down as a way of trying to cope with them. The result was one of his most distressing and disturbing books: *A Grief Observed*, published in 1961 under a false name (N.W. Clerk). *A Grief Observed* is basically an edited version of four notebooks in which Lewis kept an uncensored and unrestrained journal of his feelings following his wife's death. As *The Problem of Pain* indicates, Lewis had thought about most of the intellectual questions raised by suffering and death before. Yet nothing seems to have prepared him for the emotional firestorm that Davidman's death precipitated.

Lewis found that his own arguments in *The Problem of Pain* – such as describing suffering as 'God's megaphone' – seemed simplistic and inadequate in light of the suffering and death of his wife. Lewis seems to have realised that his earlier approach engaged with the surface of human life, not its depths.

> Where is God? . . . Go to Him when your need is desperate, when all other help is vain, and what do you find? A door slammed in your face, and a sound of bolting and double bolting on the inside. After that, silence.[18]

A Grief Observed describes what Lewis regards as a process of testing – not a testing *of God*, but a testing *of Lewis*. 'God has not been trying an experiment on my faith or love in order to find out their quality. He knew it already. It was I who didn't.'[19] Lewis's journal records his thoughts, no matter how incoherent, as he explores every option. Maybe God is a tyrant. Maybe there isn't a God at all. Yet these are not conclusions that Lewis has reached after careful analysis. They are merely options to raise and explore, thoroughly and honestly. And in the end, he rejects them. *A Grief Observed* is a narrative of the testing and maturing of faith, not simply its recovery – and certainly not its loss.

Why? There seems to be a clear tipping point in Lewis's thinking. It comes when Lewis wishes that he had been allowed to suffer, instead of his wife. 'If only I could bear it, or the worst of it, or any of it, instead of her.'[20] Lewis believes that this is the mark of the true lover – a willingness to take on pain and suffering in order that the beloved might be spared its worst. But isn't that what God did on the cross? Didn't Christ suffer on behalf of others, so that they might be spared the pain?[21] God *could* bear suffering. And God *did* bear that suffering.

Reflecting on Lewis's Approaches

So let's ask a question. What are the differences between the approaches that Lewis adopted to suffering in *The Problem of Pain* and *A Grief Observed*? The most obvious is the tone. *The Problem of Pain* is coolly logical and clinical; *A Grief Observed* is searing in its emotional intensity. It remains one of the finest explorations of the process of grieving.

To its critics, Lewis's approach in *The Problem of Pain* amounts to an evasion of the reality of evil and suffering as something that *we actually experience*; instead, suffering and evil are reduced to abstract ideas, which require being fitted into the jigsaw puzzle of faith. To read *A Grief Observed* is to realise how a rational faith can fall to pieces when it is confronted with suffering as a personal reality, rather than as a mild theoretical disturbance.

Yet what of their approaches? There is an obvious difference in tone. But what about their substance? I have to confess that I have failed to find a major difference between them at this point. Although they *feel* different, they take me to much the same intellectual conclusion. Suffering does not call into question the 'big picture' of the Christian faith. It reminds us that we do not see the whole picture and are thus unable to fit all of its pieces neatly into place. In 1940, Lewis focused on the intellectual discomfort this caused Christians; in 1961, on the emotional distress it caused them.

Lewis's close friend Austin Farrer suggested that Lewis did not really integrate faith and feelings in his earlier period. Yet this integration seems to have become increasingly important to Lewis as he grew older. Lewis realised the need to ensure that ideas and feelings, theology and the emotions, were connected to one another at a relatively late stage in his life.[22] Farrer did not see this as a particular problem. After all, some others fail to do so at all!

In both cases, Lewis's solution lies in focusing on the crucified Christ. Although the angle of approach is slightly different in each case, there is clearly a common theme. In reflecting on the crucified Christ, we are reminded that God entered into the world in order to bear suffering. It is not something that lies beyond the experience or presence of God.

I have often thought about Lewis's approaches when giving talks on apologetics. I am regularly asked to talk about suffering by questioners, and have noticed that they tend to come at it from quite different angles. Some see pain and suffering as intellectual inconveniences and want me to sort out the logical niceties for them. Others, however, experience suffering as existentially threatening and frightening. Like Job in the

Old Testament, they want reassurance that God really cares for them.

In terms of the ideas I develop, I give similar talks. But the tone of my responses to questioners is quite different. For the first, I use a tone quite similar to Lewis's *Problem of Pain*, although I note the pastoral importance of the question. For the second, I talk about the emotional distress that can be caused by pain and suffering, and mention Lewis as an example of someone who went through this experience himself – and came out on the other side. 'I didn't know that!' is almost invariably the response. 'I must read *A Grief Observed*.'

That's enough for this tea-time conversation. Pain, suffering and evil are not easy topics to discuss, partly because they raise uncomfortable questions about how much we can understand anything. Lewis gives us some important and helpful pointers in contemplating the mystery of human suffering. But the problems of pain and suffering did not go away for Lewis. Soon after Davidman's death, Lewis realised that his own days were numbered. So as we bring this book to a close, let's imagine we are having lunch with Lewis at The Trout, a riverside pub just outside Oxford. We shall look at Lewis's views on hope and heaven, and how these helped him in the final phase of his life.

8

'Further Up and Further In':
C.S. Lewis on Hope and Heaven

The Apostles themselves . . . left their mark on Earth precisely because their minds were occupied with Heaven. It is since Christians have largely ceased to think of the other world that they have become so ineffective in this. Aim at Heaven and you will get earth 'thrown in': aim at earth and you will get neither.

C.S. Lewis, *Mere Christianity*

It's our final imagined meeting with Lewis on a cold and misty day in December, at the end of Oxford's first teaching term. What better topic to end with than the Christian hope? So just what is this hope? What keeps us going in life? What enables us to journey through the shadowlands? What helps us to keep walking through the valley of the shadow of death, without giving in to despair? The answer lies in that little word *hope* – a word that meant a lot to Lewis, as we shall see.

Hope is rooted in the trustworthiness of God. As Lewis himself knew so well, God can transform the valley of the shadow of death into a gateway of hope. As the great poet John Milton, whom Lewis admired so much, once wrote, hope allows us to bid farewell to fear. Lewis offers us a 'big picture' which allows us to see things in a new way. So what does Lewis have to say about the Christian hope?

An American colleague who was visiting Oxford went to see the grave of C.S. Lewis in the churchyard of Holy Trinity, Headington Quarry. Over a cup of tea afterwards, we discussed its somewhat forbidding epitaph: 'Men must endure their going hence.' My friend was puzzled by the absence of any apparent sense of hope. The inscription seemed to speak of a passive recognition of the inevitability of death. It was an affirmation of human mortality, rather than a celebration of the hope of heaven. Wasn't Lewis a Christian? So why this melancholy motto, more suggestive of a defiant stoicism than a joyful Christianity?

As far as we can tell, Lewis had no say in the choice of this text, so we can't blame him for its sonorous tone. It was chosen by Lewis's elder brother, Warnie, who lived with Lewis in Oxford until his death. Warnie arranged the details of Lewis's funeral – not very well, as it turned out – including the text on his gravestone. It had been the Shakespearean 'text for the day' on the family calendar for 23 August 1908 – the day of their mother's death from cancer, when Lewis was nearly ten years old. Its grim realism came to express the views of the young Lewis, who became an aggressive atheist, especially when serving as an infantry officer in the Great War. Where was God in the midst of the carnage he saw all around him?

Yet as we have seen, this proved to be a phase in Lewis's development, not a final resting place. Lewis's gradual move away from atheism towards Christianity reflected his growing realisation that atheism lacked real intellectual substance and seemed imaginatively impoverished. Lewis had been haunted by a deep intuition that there had to be more to life than what his minimalist atheism allowed. Above all, he found himself reflecting on the implications of a deep and elusive sense of longing, which was heightened rather than satisfied by what he found around him.

Lewis famously termed this experience of yearning 'Joy', and came to the conclusion that it pointed to something beyond the boundaries of human knowledge and experience. 'If I find in myself a desire which no experience in this world can satisfy, the most probable explanation is that I was made for another world.'[1] A transcendent realm beyond us – what Christians call 'heaven' – would make sense of what he experienced within him and observed around him.

After Lewis's 'reconversion' in 1930, he slowly began to see heaven as more than just a way of making sense of the enigmas and puzzles of this life. It was something that brought Lewis hope. Christian hope, Lewis insisted, was not some 'form of escapism or wishful thinking', but was rather 'a continual looking forward to the eternal world'.[2] Hope is a settled state of mind, in which we see this world in its true light and look forward to our final homecoming in heaven. This theme became especially important to Lewis in his final years. Lewis would have echoed Cyprian of Carthage's famous statement that Paradise is 'our native land',[3] and shared Cyprian's hope at the thought of returning to his true homeland. Lewis would want us to share it as well.

So let's set the context for Lewis's understanding of the Christian hope by telling the story of the final part of his life.

The Shape of Lewis's Final Years

The deaths of close friends and relatives are not merely saddening and disturbing. They also remind us of our own mortality. That's the point famously made by the English poet John Donne in his 'Meditation 17'. Donne asks us to imagine hearing a funeral bell tolling. This was a familiar aspect of English life in the seventeenth century. The muffled tolling of a church bell marked a death in the local community. Naturally, people would prick up their ears at this sound and wonder who had died. Donne's point was very simple: 'Now this bell tolling softly for another, says to me, Thou must die.'

> No man is an island, entire of itself; . . . any man's death diminishes me, because I am involved in mankind, and therefore never send to know for whom the bell tolls; it tolls for thee.[4]

We have already seen how the lingering death of Lewis's mother in August 1908 shattered the security of his childhood world. Lewis was not even ten years old at the time. The death of his father in 1929 may well have helped Lewis rethink the question of God. While his writings of the period show no interest in God around the time of his father's death, the question begins to emerge as significant the following year.

Lewis formed a close friendship with Charles Williams, who became a leading member of the Inklings during the period of the Second World War. Williams's sudden and unexpected death in 1945 affected Lewis deeply. Yet most traumatic of all was the death of Joy Davidman, Lewis's wife, from cancer in 1960. As we saw in our previous meeting, this unleashed a wave of emotional despair and deep questioning on Lewis's part.

Each of these deaths, in its own way, prompted Lewis to think about his own mortality. By the time he had written *A Grief Observed*, Lewis himself was unwell, displaying symptoms of the degenerative illnesses that would eventually kill him. In June 1961, Lewis wrote to his childhood friend Arthur Greeves, thanking him for his visit that summer. Lewis had clearly enjoyed Greeves's company. Yet there was a cloud on the horizon. Lewis told Greeves that he would soon have to go into hospital for a surgical operation to deal with an enlarged prostate gland.[5] Perhaps Greeves would not have been totally surprised by this news. Lewis, he had noted during his visit, 'was looking very ill'. Something was clearly wrong with him.

Yet Lewis's doctors quickly realised that things had gone too far for any kind of medical intervention. An operation was impossible. His kidneys and heart were both failing him. His condition could only be managed; it could not be cured. Lewis was going to die. It was just a matter of time.

By the end of the summer of 1961, Lewis was so ill that he was unable to return to Cambridge University to teach. Accepting that he might not live much longer, Lewis drew up his will in November of that year. His doctors were able to stabilise his condition by the spring of the following year, allowing him to resume teaching at Cambridge until June 1963. Encouraged by how things seemed to be going, Lewis arranged to return to Ireland to visit Arthur Greeves. He never made that trip.

When Walter Hooper, who got to know Lewis around this time, arrived at The Kilns on the morning of Sunday 14 July to take Lewis to church, he found Lewis seriously unwell. Lewis was exhausted, scarcely able to hold a cup of tea in his hands, and seemed to be in a state of confusion. Lewis went into an Oxford nursing home the next day, suffered a heart attack almost immediately after his arrival, fell into a coma, and was judged to be close to death.

He recovered enough to be discharged. However, Lewis had no doubts about the inevitable outcome of his rapid decline. With great sadness, he resigned from his Cambridge chair and prepared to spend whatever time remained to him at home at The Kilns. Lewis later told his friends that he wished he had died during his coma at the nursing home. The experience, he later wrote to a friend, was 'very gentle'. It seemed a shame, 'having reached the gate so easily, not to be allowed through'.[6] Like Lazarus, he would have to go through the experience again. And it might not be so pleasant or easy the next time.

Lewis died at home at The Kilns on 22 November 1963. There were no warning signs. Warnie noted that Lewis seemed a little tired after lunch, and suggested that he should go to bed. At four o'clock that afternoon, Warnie brought him a cup of tea and found him 'drowsy but comfortable'. Shortly afterwards, Warnie heard a crash from Lewis's bedroom. He ran in to find that Lewis had collapsed and was lying unconscious at the foot of the bed. His death certificate would give the multiple causes of his death as renal failure, prostate obstruction and cardiac degeneration. A few hours later, the world learned that President John F. Kennedy had been assassinated in Dallas, Texas.

Warnie was overwhelmed by his brother's death and sought refuge in drinking large quantities of whisky. While he spent 26 November in bed, recovering from excessive alcohol intake, a small group of friends and colleagues gathered on a cold frosty morning to bury Lewis at Holy Trinity Church, Headington Quarry, Oxford.

During the summer of 1963, Lewis had written a number of letters dealing with what he believed to be his imminent death. The theme of hope predominates.

As we noted, the rather melancholic text Warnie chose for his brother's gravestone was 'Men must endure their going hence'. Yet some of Lewis's own words, written a few months earlier to an American correspondent, express both his style and his hope in the face of his looming death rather better than the somewhat severe and forbidding epitaph chosen by his brother. We are, Lewis suggested, like

> a seed waiting in the good earth: waiting to come up a flower in the Gardener's good time, up into the *real* world, the real waking. I suppose that our whole present life, looked back on from there, will seem only a drowsy half-waking. We are here in the land of dreams. But cock-crow is coming.[7]

So let's explore Lewis's views on the hope of heaven. It's a very appropriate way to end our series of imaginary encounters. As this is going to be our final meeting, we're going to be a little more critical than usual. We're going to look at some concerns related to Lewis's ideas about heaven, and see what he would say in response.

Lewis's Views on Heaven: Some Misgivings

Let's open by looking at some words that Lewis wrote in his autobiography, *Surprised by Joy*: 'It is more important that Heaven should exist than that any of us should reach it.'[8] Many of Lewis's readers find this idea perplexing – especially when Lewis commented that he still held that view 'most strongly'. Why did Lewis think that the mere existence of heaven is more important than any hope of entering it? Let's ask Lewis to unpack his meaning, and see if we can make sense of what he is saying.

Lewis developed this idea during the period of his 'New Look' – the time during the 1920s when he was trying to sort himself out intellectually.[9] Lewis became interested in a form of philosophical idealism which emphasised the importance of a transcendent dimension to life, or the recognition of a transcendent principle. That's one of the core themes of his 'argument from morality'. Unless there is some transcendent ground of justice – which we find, of course, in the Christian doctrine of God – then our notions of justice are simply human inventions, reflecting the views of those with power and influence.

Now, most of us will agree with Lewis on this point. Indeed, it is a very powerful apologetic argument, which has been rejected but not refuted by some irritated atheists. Yet we still feel uneasy. We can agree with Lewis about the importance of a transcendent being or place. But surely there is more to the Christian view of heaven than just accepting that it exists!

There is a serious issue here. Many scholars have argued that Lewis's early vision of heaven was perhaps as much Platonic as it was Christian.[10] For example, consider the words that Lewis places in the mouth of Lord Digory towards the end of *The Last Battle*: 'It's all in Plato, all in Plato: bless me, what *do* they teach them at these schools!'[11] Lord Digory is trying to explain that the 'Old Narnia', which had a historical beginning and end, was really 'only a shadow or a copy of the real Narnia which has always been here and always will be here'.[12] A central theme of many of Lewis's writings is that we live in a world that is a 'bright shadow' of something greater and better. The present world is a 'copy' or 'shadow' of a real world. The old Narnia was a shadow or a copy of the 'new Narnia' or the 'real Narnia', just as England and our world are shadows or copies of something in heaven.

Lewis seems to have understood the idea of heaven as a kind of sense-making device which helped to give coherence to the world of thought and experience. For most of the 1940s and 1950s, Lewis exulted primarily in the ability of the Christian faith to make sense of reality. Christianity gave coherence to the world. It helped us realise that there is a big picture which makes sense of the snapshots. And, as Lewis showed us in the Chronicles of Narnia, Christianity tells a 'big story' that allows us to see our own story in a new way.

Let's look at Plato's ideas in a little more detail. We've already looked at the analogy that appealed so much to Lewis – the people in the cave (see page 68). The unfortunate inhabitants of the dark, smoky cave think it is the only world. As far as they are concerned, there is nothing beyond it. But what if there is a world beyond the cave? If there is such a world, we would see the cave in a very different way. We would realise that we live in a very limited world of shadows and smoke.

That's why Lewis uses the image of God as a 'sun' that lights up the world. Or heaven as a realm beyond the limits of present human experience, yet which our deepest intuitions and experiences have pointed us towards. Occasionally these realities break into our dark world – like light through the chinks of the Second World War blackout curtains (see pages 143–4) – brightening our minds with the truth. Glimpsing them is like hearing the sound of music faintly, coming from across the distant hills. Or catching the scent of a far-off flower, wafted by a passing breeze. Lewis came to see such experiences as 'arrows of Joy', wake-up calls to discover and experience a deeper vision of reality. Yet this picture is rather different from the New Testament's idea of heaven as an utter transformation of this world, which takes place at the end of time!

The New Testament develops two interrelated themes. First, the Christian faith shows us the way things really are. This is about *revelation*, coming to see things properly. But revelation alone doesn't change our situation. Christianity doesn't just tell us that we are sinful; it offers forgiveness. It doesn't just tell us that we are in prison; it throws open the doors so that we can go free. This is what the New Testament calls *salvation*, the second theme. To use a medical analogy, the gospel offers both diagnosis (revelation) and cure (salvation). It helps us to grasp our true situation, but it also declares that our situation can be transformed, and it makes that transformation possible.

At many points in his writings, Lewis tends to think of Christianity as a means of intellectual transformation. Christianity helps us to see things as they really are. Now that's an important part of the Christian faith. And we can probably understand why an Oxford academic such as Lewis would warm to the idea of the intellectual enrichment brought to life by the Christian faith. But there's a lot more to the gospel than this!

So how might Lewis respond to these concerns? Let's find out.

Lewis's Rich Understanding of Heaven

Lewis would concede that the concerns we have just noted are fair. Yet he would ask us to appreciate that his understanding of heaven is richer and deeper than our discussion suggests. He makes this point clear in *Miracles*, one of his most meticulously argued books. Let's look at what he says there.

We need to get away from the ridiculous idea that heaven is nothing more than eternal harp playing! There are three main ways in which we use the word *heaven*, Lewis explains. The first sense of the word is 'the unconditioned Divine Life beyond all worlds'.[13] *Heaven* here means something like 'Utter Reality' or 'reality itself'. This is the notion of heaven to which Lewis refers when he declares, 'It is more important that Heaven should exist than that any of us should reach it.' There really is an ultimate reality. How we get into it is a secondary question. If there is no ultimate reality, it's pointless to think about how we might get there.

But Lewis would want to caution us at this point. We naturally think of heaven as a place – a *somewhere*. Yet Lewis points out that while this may be the way in which we think of heaven, it is not the way heaven really is. Heaven is totally non-spatial and non-temporal. Even saying that heaven is 'where' God is shows that we need spatial images to think about heaven. But it's not a place. It's ultimate reality – something so great that we just can't take it in properly, and have to use images based on the world that we know. So we think of heaven as a place, simply because that's the only analogy that lies to hand.

The second sense of heaven is being in the presence of God. In this sense, we can think of heaven as our 'true country', even though it isn't really a 'country' at all. Heaven is about being with God, not necessarily about being with God *in a specific place*. Once more, Lewis emphasises how dependent we are on images to visualise heaven, and how this leads us to assume that it is a 'place'.

Finally, Lewis identifies a third sense of heaven – the place in which our new bodies will live after the resurrection. Once more, Lewis notes that we simply cannot avoid using spatial language to speak about heaven. We think of it as the place where God is, and the place where we shall one day be as well. Yet Lewis makes it clear at a number of points that it is only the created order that is characterised by time and space. To be in heaven is to step outside a world of space and time into eternity – a timeless place, which we find virtually impossible to think of, except in terms of images of places.

Now that Lewis has set out his rich vision of heaven, it's easy to see how its three components are linked together. Yet by the 1940s, Lewis had embraced a deeper vision of heaven. While he never lost sight of the idea that heaven helps us make sense of what we experience and observe on earth, the idea of entering heaven and experiencing its joy became increasingly important to him. Some lines from *The Last Battle*, the concluding novel of the Chronicles of Narnia, capture this point particularly well. On seeing the 'new Narnia', the Unicorn declares: 'I have come home at last! This is my real country! I belong here. This is the land I have been looking for all my life, though I never knew it till now.'[14] For Lewis, the Christian hope is about returning home to where we really belong.

Does this mean that Lewis exults in death? Is he a 'world-denying' writer, who treats this world as devoid of value? No. For Lewis, this world is where we have been placed. It is God's world, and is to be valued, appreciated and enjoyed. Yet it is studded with clues that it is not our real home, that there is a still better world beyond its frontiers, that one may dare to hope to enter and inhabit this better place. Lewis affirms the delight, joy and purposefulness of life. He asks us to realise that, when this finally comes to an end, something even better awaits us.

One of the best statements of Lewis's view about the Christian hope is found in the 1941 sermon 'The Weight of Glory'. Lewis explains that our imaginations have been taken captive by a lie. As we discovered in an earlier meeting with Lewis, he was deeply concerned that his generation had come to believe that the notion of transcendent realms or of worlds to come was simply illusion, which could not be taken seriously by modern educated people. Heaven is so yesterday. We now know (or so we are told) that the true destiny of humanity is 'found on this earth'[15] – and nowhere else.

Lewis demands that we protest against this distorted and degraded vision of life, and help people break free of its lure. The Christian churches need to break this spell and liberate the world from this demeaning and impoverishing belief, which is presented as if it were fact. The secular world offers people only a hopeless end; instead, Lewis wants them to see and grasp the endless hope of the Christian faith and live in its light.

To 'aim at Heaven', as Lewis says in *Mere Christianity*, is not to neglect this world or earthly concerns. Rather, it is to raise our horizon and elevate our expectations – and then to behave on earth in the light of this greater reality. We must infuse earth with the fragrance of heaven. The true believer is not someone who disengages from this world in order to focus on heaven, but rather the one who tries to make this world more like heaven. Lewis is surely right here. The Christian vision of heaven has driven many to improve this world. 'The

Christians who did most for the present world were just those who thought most of the next.'[16]

Lewis is no killjoy. He does not ask us to deny that we experience desire in this life, nor does he suggest that these desires are evil or a distraction from the real business of life. His point is that our desires cannot be, and were never meant to be, satisfied by earthly pleasures alone. They are 'good images' or signposts of something 'further up and further in'. They are foretastes of the true source of satisfaction that we will find in the presence of God. For Lewis, heaven is the 'other country' for which we were created in the first place. We should 'make it the main object of life to press on to that other country and to help others do the same'.[17]

So what happens if we get things wrong? What if we fail to realise that something we really value and love is a 'copy, or echo, or mirage' of something heavenly, and confuse 'the thing itself' with what it suggests? Lewis leaves us in little doubt. We will become frustrated and cynical. We turn a good signpost into a false idol, confusing a sign with what it points to. And when a pleasure is corrupted in this kind of way, it ends up a vice.

This is our last imagined meeting with Lewis. What parting thought would Lewis leave with us? There are so many things he might say. He might suggest that we imagine the most delightful experience we have ever had, and then tell us that heaven is just like that – only bigger and better. But I think he might leave us with the thought that we find towards the end of *The Last Battle*. Like many other Christian writers before him, Lewis declares that the hope of heaven enables us to see this world in its true perspective. This life is the preparation for that greater reality. It is but the cover and title page of the 'Great Story', in which every chapter is 'better than the one before'.[18]

For Lewis, we are part of that 'Great Story'. Our own stories are given new meaning and value when they are woven into the greater story of God, and when we discover that each of us is 'a real ingredient in the divine happiness'.[19] Lewis's final challenge to us might be this: What is your role in that story? And are you playing it to the full? And with those words, Lewis would leave us, putting on his hat and coat, and heading into the misty distance as he walked back to Oxford.

As he finally disappeared from view in the fading winter sunlight, we might reflect on the way in which Lewis found his own place in that 'Great Story'. In the early 1920s, Lewis hoped to be remembered as an atheist poet, whose bitter and forceful condemnations of an uncaring and absent God would rid the world of any lingering religious belief. Today, he is remembered as one of the greatest Christian apologists of all time. He has become an ingredient of that greater story, and an encouragement to us to find our own place.

Lewis: The Legacy

When my biography of Lewis was published in 2013, I began to receive a large number of letters and messages. Some expressed delight about the biography. A few suggested some helpful corrections. Some writers told me about their own experiences of Lewis. But the vast majority were about the impact that Lewis had had on the writers. These people wanted to share with me the way in which Lewis had transformed and enriched their lives, especially their faith. Lewis himself would have had no idea of how significant an influence he would be for so many after his death.

So as we end this series of conversations, let us appreciate that Lewis is not simply someone who helps us think about our faith. He is someone who challenges us to think about the difference that we make to others – the memories we will leave behind us, and lives that are changed through our influence. Only now can we begin to appreciate the full extent of Lewis's legacy. But what will ours be? Who will remember us? And why?

When I was researching my biography of Lewis, I came across many photographs of Lewis and his friends from the 1910s and 1920s. Some showed Lewis in small groups of people; others in larger gatherings. It was easy to identify Lewis himself and some of those who played an important role in his life – such as his father, his brother and his childhood friend Arthur Greeves. But time after time, I could not identify some of the other people in the photographs. Nor could any of those I consulted, who had expert knowledge of Lewis's family history. All too often, I had to pencil the word 'unknown' against my copies of these images. Whoever these people were, we do not know their names. We probably never will.

Yet it was obvious from the photographs that they were important members of Lewis's circle of family and friends. Once they mattered; now they were forgotten, reduced to anonymous traces on photographic paper. Their memory and identity had simply faded out of history, like the ink on a piece of writing paper being washed away by a spilled glass of water. Memory is fragile. We are so easily forgotten. Lewis is one of the few who have left footprints on history – footprints by which he will be remembered.

Yet Lewis himself might helpfully remind us at this point that the most important thing is that each of us, whether remembered by others or not, is remembered by God. And that's what really matters. Human history may forget about us, as it has forgotten so many. But our names are engraved on God's hands and written in the Book of Life – a fitting, even inspiring, thought with which to end our series of conversations with Lewis about the meaning of life.

ACKNOWLEDGEMENTS

The author and publishers gratefully acknowledge permission to reproduce extracts from copyrighted material, as follows. *Collected Letters* by C.S. Lewis, copyright © C.S. Lewis Pte. Ltd 2004, 2006; *Surprised by Joy* by C.S. Lewis, copyright © C.S. Lewis Pte. Ltd 1955; *Essays* by C.S. Lewis, copyright © C.S. Lewis Pte. Ltd 2000; *Mere Christianity* by C.S. Lewis, copyright © C.S. Lewis Pte. Ltd 1942, 1943, 1944, 1952; *The Lion, the Witch and the Wardrobe* by C.S. Lewis, copyright © C.S. Lewis Pte. Ltd 1950; *The Silver Chair* by C.S. Lewis, copyright © C.S. Lewis Pte. Ltd 1953; *The Last Battle* by C.S. Lewis, copyright © C.S. Lewis Pte. Ltd 1956; *The Magician's Nephew* by C.S. Lewis, copyright © C.S. Lewis Pte. Ltd 1955; *The Pilgrim's Regress* by C.S. Lewis, copyright © C.S. Lewis Pte. Ltd 1933; *The Problem of Pain* by C.S. Lewis, copyright © C.S. Lewis Pte. Ltd 1940; *A Grief Observed* by C.S. Lewis, copyright © C.S. Lewis Pte. Ltd 1961.

For Further Reading

The best biographies of Lewis are the following:

Jacobs, Alan, *The Narnian: The Life and Imagination of C.S. Lewis* (London: SPCK, 2005).

McGrath, Alister E., *C.S. Lewis – A Life: Eccentric Genius, Reluctant Prophet* (London: Hodder & Stoughton, 2013).

Sayer, George, *Jack: A Life of C.S. Lewis* (London: Hodder & Stoughton, 2005).

Works about Lewis that are relevant to this book follow:

Aeschliman, Michael D., *The Restitution of Man: C.S. Lewis and the Case against Scientism* (Grand Rapids, MI: Eerdmans, 1998).

Carnell, Corbin Scott, *Bright Shadow of Reality: Spiritual Longing in C.S. Lewis* (Grand Rapids, MI: Eerdmans, 1999).

Carpenter, Humphrey, *The Inklings: C.S. Lewis, J.R.R.*

Tolkien, Charles Williams, and Their Friends (London: Allen & Unwin, 1981).

Downing, David C., *Into the Wardrobe: C.S. Lewis and the Narnia Chronicles* (San Francisco: Jossey-Bass, 2005).

Duriez, Colin, *C.S. Lewis: A Biography of Friendship* (Oxford: Lion Books, 2013).

Glyer, Diana, *The Company They Keep: C.S. Lewis and J.R.R. Tolkien as Writers in Community* (Kent, OH: Kent State University Press, 2007).

Heck, Joel D., *Irrigating Deserts: C.S. Lewis on Education* (St Louis, MO: Concordia, 2005).

Hooper, Walter, *C.S. Lewis: The Companion and Guide* (London: HarperCollins, 2005).

MacSwain, Robert, and Michael Ward (eds), *The Cambridge Companion to C.S. Lewis* (Cambridge: Cambridge University Press, 2010).

Markos, Louis, *On the Shoulders of Hobbits: The Road to Virtue with Tolkien and Lewis* (Chicago: Moody, 2012).

McGrath, Alister E., *The Intellectual World of C.S. Lewis* (Oxford and Malden, MA: Wiley-Blackwell, 2013).

Meilander, Gilbert, *The Taste for the Other: The Social and Ethical Thought of C.S. Lewis* (Grand Rapids, MI: Eerdmans, 1998).

Nicholi, Armand M., *The Question of God: C.S. Lewis and Sigmund Freud Debate God, Love, Sex, and the Meaning of Life* (New York: Free Press, 2002).

Ward, Michael, *Planet Narnia: The Seven Heavens in the*

Imagination of C.S. Lewis (Oxford: Oxford University Press, 2008).

Williams, Rowan D., *The Lion's World: A Journey into the Heart of Narnia* (London: SPCK, 2013).

Editions of works by Lewis referenced in this work follow:

The Abolition of Man (New York: HarperCollins, 2001).

The Chronicles of Narnia, 7 vols (London: Harper-Collins, 2002).

The Collected Letters of C.S. Lewis, ed. Walter Hooper, 3 vols (San Francisco: HarperOne, 2004–6).

Essay Collection and Other Short Pieces, ed. Lesley Walmsley (London: HarperCollins, 2000).

An Experiment in Criticism (Cambridge: Cambridge University Press, 1992).

The Four Loves (London: HarperCollins, 2002).

A Grief Observed (London: HarperCollins, 1994). [Originally published under the pseudonym N.W. Clerk.]

Mere Christianity (London: HarperCollins, 2002).

The Problem of Pain (London: HarperCollins, 2002).

Surprised by Joy (London: HarperCollins, 2002).

Chapter 1: The Grand Panorama: C.S. Lewis on the Meaning of Life

Lewis sets out the ability of Christianity to make sense of things at several points in his works. The best starting point is *Mere Christianity*, especially Book 1, chapters 1–4, and Book 3, chapter 10.

The essay 'Is theology poetry?' repays study:
'Is theology poetry?', in *Essay Collection*, 10–21.

For a discussion of how Lewis came to discover
Christianity, see the following:
Downing, David C., *The Most Reluctant Convert: C.S.
Lewis's Journey to Faith* (Downers Grove, IL:
InterVarsity Press, 2002).
McGrath, Alister E., *C.S. Lewis – A Life: Eccentric
Genius, Reluctant Prophet* (London: Hodder &
Stoughton, 2013), 131–59.

Chapter 2: 'Old Friends to Trust': C.S. Lewis on Friendship

Lewis's most extended discussion of friendship is found
in the fourth chapter of *The Four Loves*.

For the best study of the Inklings, see the following:
Carpenter, Humphrey, *The Inklings: C.S. Lewis, J.R.R.
Tolkien, Charles Williams, and Their Friends* (London:
Allen & Unwin, 1978).

For the way in which the Inklings worked, see the
following:
Glyer, Diana, *The Company They Keep: C.S. Lewis
and J.R.R. Tolkien as Writers in Community* (Kent,
OH: Kent State University Press, 2007).

For reflections on the significance of the friendship
between Lewis and Tolkien, see the following:

Duriez, Colin, *C.S. Lewis: A Biography of Friendship* (Oxford: Lion Books, 2013).

Jacobs, Alan, 'The End of Friendship', in *Wayfaring: Essays Pleasant and Unpleasant* (Grand Rapids, MI: Eerdmans, 2010), 128–36.

For an assessment of Lewis's approach to friendship and love, see the following:

Leiva-Merikakis, Erasmo, *Love's Sacred Order: The Four Loves Revisited* (San Francisco: Ignatius Press, 2000).

Chapter 3: A Story-Shaped World: C.S. Lewis on Narnia and the Importance of Stories

To get the most out of this chapter, you should read the following books:

The Lion, the Witch and the Wardrobe
The Voyage of the Dawn Treader

On the writing and themes of Narnia, see the following:

Brown, Devon, *Inside Narnia: A Guide to Exploring 'The Lion, the Witch and the Wardrobe'* (Grand Rapids, MI: Baker, 2005).

Downing, David C., *Into the Wardrobe: C.S. Lewis and the Narnia Chronicles* (San Francisco: Jossey-Bass, 2005).

Jacobs, Alan, *The Narnian: The Life and Imagination of C.S. Lewis* (London: SPCK, 2005).

Williams, Rowan D., *The Lion's World: A Journey into the Heart of Narnia* (London: SPCK, 2012).

Chapter 4: The Lord and the Lion: C.S. Lewis on Aslan and the Christian Life

To get the most out of this chapter, you should read the following books (in this order):
The Lion, the Witch and the Wardrobe
The Magician's Nephew
The Last Battle

Other works that you may find helpful are the following:

Alexander, Joy, '"The Whole Art and Joy of Words": Aslan's Speech in the Chronicles of Narnia', *Mythlore* 91 (2003): 37–48.

Hauerwas, Stanley, 'Aslan and the New Morality', *Religious Education* 67, no. 6 (1972): 419–29.

Markos, Louis, *On the Shoulders of Hobbits: The Road to Virtue with Tolkien and Lewis* (Chicago: Moody, 2012).

Williams, Rowan D., *The Lion's World: A Journey into the Heart of Narnia* (New York: Oxford University Press, 2013), 49–111.

Chapter 5: Talking about Faith: C.S. Lewis on the Art of Apologetics

Lewis's best apologetic work is *Mere Christianity*, which is an edited version of his Broadcast Talks given for the BBC during the Second World War. I especially recommend that you read its first five chapters, which set out Lewis's version of the 'argument from morality'.

On Lewis's approach to apologetics, see the following:

McGrath, Alister E., 'Reason, Experience, and Imagination: Lewis's Apologetic Method', in *The Intellectual World of C.S. Lewis* (Oxford and Malden, MA: Wiley-Blackwell, 2013), 129–46.

Walsh, Chad, *C.S. Lewis: Apostle to the Skeptics* (New York: Macmillan, 1949). This is a classic study, which first introduced many Americans to Lewis, and is still valuable.

Ward, Michael, 'The Good Serves the Better and Both the Best: C.S. Lewis on Imagination and Reason in Apologetics', in *Imaginative Apologetics: Theology, Philosophy, and the Catholic Tradition*, ed. Andrew Davison (London: SCM Press, 2012), 59–78.

Lewis has had a very significant impact on recent Christian apologetics, as can be seen from the following works:

McGrath, Alister E., *Mere Apologetics: How to Help Seekers and Skeptics Find Faith* (Grand Rapids, MI: Baker Books, 2012).

Sire, James W., *A Little Primer on Humble Apologetics* (Downers Grove, IL: InterVarsity Press, 2006).

Wright, N.T., *Simply Christian: Why Christianity Makes Sense* (London: SPCK, 2010).

Chapter 6: A Love of Learning: C.S. Lewis on Education

Lewis's views on the shortcomings of modern education are set out particularly clearly in *The Abolition of Man*, especially its first chapter.

His essay 'On the Reading of Old Books' is a classic, and well worth reading. See Lesley Walmsley (ed.), *Essay Collection and Other Short Pieces* (London: HarperCollins, 2000), 438–43.

For Lewis's career as an educationalist, see the following:

McGrath, Alister E., *C.S. Lewis – A Life: Eccentric Genius, Reluctant Prophet* (London: Hodder & Stoughton, 2013), 161–90.

For Lewis's views on education and their contemporary relevance, see the following:

Heck, Joel D., *Irrigating Deserts: C.S. Lewis on Education* (St Louis, MO: Concordia, 2005).

Chapter 7: Coping with Suffering: C.S. Lewis on the Problem of Pain

Lewis's views on pain and suffering are best studied from these two works:

The Problem of Pain

A Grief Observed

Other works that you may find helpful:

Keller, Timothy, *Walking with God through Pain and Suffering* (London: Hodder & Stoughton, 2013).

McGrath, Alister E., 'The Cross, Suffering, and Theological Bewilderment: Reflections on Martin Luther and C.S. Lewis', in *Mere Theology: Christian Faith and the Discipleship of the Mind* (London: SPCK, 2010), 39–50.

Root, Jerry, *C.S. Lewis and a Problem of Evil* (Eugene, OR: Pickwick Publications, 2009).

Ward, Michael, 'On Suffering', in *The Cambridge Companion to C.S. Lewis*, ed. Robert MacSwain and Michael Ward (Cambridge: Cambridge University Press, 2010), 203–19.

Chapter 8: 'Further Up and Further In': C.S. Lewis on Hope and Heaven

For Lewis's views on heaven and the Christian hope, you should read the following:

Mere Christianity, Book 3, chapter 10.

Miracles, chapter 16.

'The Weight of Glory', in Lesley Walmsley (ed.), *Essay Collection and Other Short Pieces* (London: HarperCollins, 2000), 96–106.

Other works that you may find helpful are the following:

Connolly, Sean, *Inklings of Heaven: C.S. Lewis and Eschatology* (Leominster, Herefordshire: Gracewing, 2007).

Edwards, Michael, 'C.S. Lewis: Imagining Heaven', in *Literature and Theology* 6 (1992): 107–24.

Urang, Gunnar, *Shadows of Heaven: Religion and Fantasy in the Writing of C.S. Lewis, Charles Williams, and J.R.R. Tolkien* (Philadelphia: Pilgrim Press, 1971).

Willis, John Randolph, *Pleasures Forevermore: The Theology of C.S. Lewis* (Chicago: Loyola University Press, 1983).

Introducing Lewis

'Just who is C.S. Lewis?' I asked one of my schoolmates at my high school in Belfast back in the late 1960s. Our headmaster had mentioned how much he had enjoyed reading one of Lewis's books, which had something to do with a lion and a wardrobe. It seemed an improbable plotline, and I wondered what on earth it was all about. It was not the most promising introduction to Lewis, and my momentary interest in him went no further. I was too preoccupied with studying science to worry much about lions or wardrobes.

At that stage, I was a rather ungracious and aggressive sixteen-year-old atheist, who took the view that science had long since eliminated belief in God. It was, therefore, something of a surprise when I found my intellectual world turned inside out only a few years later. I had gone up to Oxford University to study science in much greater detail, assuming it would confirm my atheism. After much mental anguish, I realised that Christianity made far more sense than atheism. Much to my embarrassment, I became one of a group of people whom I had, until this point, totally despised – serious religious believers.

As I began to think about my faith, friends suggested I should read C.S. Lewis. Curious, I bought a few of his books in 1974, and scribbled the date of purchase on their title pages. They have remained with me ever since. It's hard to put into words what I found in Lewis then, and continue to find to this day. Somehow, he seemed to present Christianity in a way that satisfied my intellectual longings and stimulated my imagination. It wasn't just that he said some good things; he also seemed to say them rather well.

Forty years later, I still read Lewis. Indeed, I keep coming back to him, finding many things I have previously missed. There always seems to be added layers of meaning waiting to be discovered, good images to be used in sermons, or elegant turns of phrase to be considered and savoured. I am hardly alone in this evaluation. Lewis was one of the most widely read religious writers of the twentieth century.

So who was C.S. Lewis? Clive Staples Lewis was born in Belfast on 29 November 1898. His father was a successful lawyer, who was doing well enough to allow the family to move to a large house (affectionately known as 'Little Lea') on the outskirts of Belfast in 1905. By the time Lewis had settled into this new house, he asked his family to call him 'Jack'. Nobody really knows why. Lewis and his older brother, Warnie, spent hours alone in the vast attic of the old house, inhabiting imaginary worlds of their own making. There were, Lewis recalled, books everywhere in the house. Both his father and mother read widely, and Lewis was free to roam and read as he pleased. When Warnie left home to go to school in England, Lewis took to reading on his own, developing a vivid sense of imagination and longing.

While waiting for Warnie to come home from school during vacations, Lewis used his imagination to create new worlds. From the windows of Little Lea, the young Lewis could see the distant Castlereagh Hills. These far-off hills seemed to symbolise something that lay beyond his reach. A sense of intense longing arose as he contemplated them. Although Lewis could not say exactly *what* he longed for, the mysterious hills seemed to heighten his yearning rather than satisfy it.

Yet tragedy was about to strike the Lewis family. Lewis's mother, Flora, died of cancer in August 1908, ending the security of his childhood. As he later recalled, 'It was sea and islands now; the great continent had sunk like Atlantis.' Albert Lewis decided it would be best if his younger son went to boarding schools in England – Wynyard School, Watford; then Cherbourg School, Malvern; and finally Malvern College. None of these worked out well. Lewis became deeply unhappy, unable to cope with the pressures of school life. Eventually, Albert Lewis realised that things were not working out for his younger son. He would have to do something about it.

In the end, Albert Lewis hit on a brilliant solution. Warnie had set his heart on a military career in the

British army. But there was a problem. Warnie had been thrown out of his school for smoking. His father realised he would have to provide some private tuition to make sure his son passed the entrance examinations for the army. And he knew whom he wanted to teach him.

William T. Kirkpatrick, Albert Lewis's former head-master, had gained a formidable reputation as an educationalist in Ireland. By this time Kirkpatrick had retired, and had time on his hands. Albert Lewis asked him if he would tutor Warnie. This worked so well that Warnie ended up in the top 10 per cent of candidates in the entrance examinations for the Royal Military Academy at Sandhurst, Britain's premier institution for the training of future army officers.

When it became painfully obvious that his younger son wasn't coping with school, Albert Lewis asked Kirkpatrick to tutor his younger son as well. He knew he was taking a risk. But it soon became clear that he had hit on a brilliant solution. Lewis was sent to study with Kirkpatrick, who then lived in Surrey. Lewis flourished in his new environment. Kirkpatrick was able to give Lewis the close personal attention he needed. Kirkpatrick introduced Lewis to the Oxford tutorial model, forcing him to develop and defend his views. Thanks to Kirkpatrick's teaching methods, Lewis won a scholarship to University College, Oxford, to study classics in December 1916. It was an outstanding achievement.

By this time, Lewis had become a hardened atheist. His letters of this period make it clear that this was not an adolescent reaction against the faith of his parents, but a considered rejection of belief in God based on arguments that he believed to be unanswerable. No thinking person, he asserted, could seriously believe in God. Lewis's dogmatic atheism caused concern to his closest friend, Arthur Greeves, a committed Christian. Lewis later recalled that he 'bombarded' Greeves with 'all the thin artillery of a seventeen year old rationalist'. In the end, the differences between Greeves and Lewis on this matter were so great that they simply agreed no longer to discuss the matter in their letters.

In August 1914, the First World War broke out. By the time Lewis won a place at Oxford University, the 'Great War' (as it was known at the time) was in its third year. Lewis realised it was inevitable that he would have to go to war. Lewis volunteered to enlist in the British army, rather than wait to be conscripted.

Lewis was demobilised in December 1918 and resumed his studies at University College, Oxford, in January 1919. He began by studying classics. Oxford quickly realised that Lewis was a brilliant student. He was awarded First Class Honours in classical moderations (the first part of Oxford's classics course) in 1920, and First Class Honours in *Literae Humaniores* (a Latin phrase meaning 'humane letters', the second part of the course) in 1922. On realising that he needed to widen his academic competency in order to secure a teaching position, Lewis spent the next year gaining First Class Honours in English Language and Literature, cramming two years of studies into a single year. Lewis had gained what Oxford called a 'triple first' – a highly distinguished academic accolade.

But there was no job for him at the end of his studies. Lewis managed to get a temporary lectureship in philosophy at University College for the academic year 1923–24. Finally, he was appointed to a tutorial fellowship in English Language and Literature at Magdalen College, Oxford, in 1925. Lewis now became a member of the Oxford University Faculty of English Language and Literature, where he developed a growing friendship with J.R.R. Tolkien, playing a key role in encouraging Tolkien to complete and publish the classic work now known as *The Lord of the Rings*.

Although Lewis was still an atheist when he took up his fellowship at Magdalen College in 1925, he was clearly in the process of questioning his dogmatic godlessness. Lewis increasingly came to find a godless world uninteresting and unpersuasive. His reading of English literature persuaded him that believing in God was far more interesting and persuasive than atheism. He wrote in his autobiography, 'A young man who wishes to remain a sound Atheist cannot be too careful of his reading. There are traps everywhere.' In the end, Lewis found himself overwhelmed by his growing realisation of the reality of God, becoming 'the most dejected and reluctant convert in all England'.

Lewis now believed in God. Yet there was a second phase to his conversion, which began in September 1931. At this time Lewis was moving from a generalised belief in God to a specific commitment to Christianity.

Lewis's conversion to Christianity – which he later described in *Surprised by Joy* (1955) – initially had little impact on his academic career. His first academic book, *The Allegory of Love* (1936), had been well received, winning the Sir Israel Gollancz Memorial Prize in 1937. The publication of this work marked the beginning of his inexorable rise to academic fame, sealed with his magisterial *English Literature in the Sixteenth Century* (1954) and his election as a Fellow of the British Academy. Other academic landmarks along the way included the 1941 Ballard Matthews Lectures at University College, Bangor (published as *A Preface to 'Paradise Lost'*); the 1943 Riddell Memorial Lectures (published as *The Abolition of Man*); and his election as a Fellow of the Royal Society of Literature in 1948.

Yet these heavyweight academic works – though widely read and respected in their time – are not the reason that Lewis is remembered today. Alongside his scholarly writings, Lewis wrote books of a very different nature. Aiming at clarity and conviction, Lewis produced a series of works to communicate the reasonableness of Christianity to his own generation. He had once been an atheist himself. So why not try to explain and commend his new faith to those who had yet to discover God? These works brought him popular acclaim, but seemed to some to destroy his scholarly reputation. In the late 1940s, Lewis was passed over for a series of senior academic appointments at Oxford, including the Merton professorship of English Literature.

Lewis's first popular book, *The Pilgrim's Regress* (1933), was based loosely on John Bunyan's classic *The Pilgrim's Progress*. It was not a success. Nevertheless, Lewis continued to write at a popular level. *The Problem of Pain*, which appeared in 1940, was well received. On the basis of its clarity and intelligence of argument, Lewis was invited by the BBC to give a series of radio talks about Christianity. These were so successful that he gave three more series of talks, which were brought together in the classic work *Mere Christianity* (1952). In 1942, Lewis published *The Screwtape Letters*, whose wit and insight firmly established Lewis's reputation as a leading defender of the Christian faith, especially in the United States.

That reputation was consolidated by further works, including *The Great Divorce* (1945) and *Miracles* (1947). Outspokenly critical of 'Christianity-and-water' (as he dubbed liberal versions of Christianity), he struck a deep chord of sympathy with his readers. His critics were furious. The British journalist Alistair Cooke, for example, described him as a 'very unremarkable minor prophet' who would soon be forgotten once the Second World War had ended. It was an unwise prediction, which merely showed that Cooke was himself a rather pompous and incompetent minor prophet.

Lewis's wartime fame might indeed have faded away had he not developed a quite unexpected line of writing, which took most of his close friends and family by surprise. In October 1950, the first of the seven Chronicles of Narnia appeared. *The Lion, the Witch and the Wardrobe* became a children's classic, showing Lewis's remarkable ability to engage the imagination and use it to open up some of life's great questions – such as the existence of God and the doctrine of the incarnation. Aslan, the great and noble lion of Narnia, became one of the most firmly established literary characters of the twentieth century.

By the time the final novel in the series – *The Last Battle* – was published in 1956, Lewis had left Oxford University. He had been elected as the first holder of the University of Cambridge's newly established Chair in Medieval and Renaissance English in 1954, and took up the position in January 1955. Although Lewis still lived in his Oxford home, The Kilns, at weekends, he now lived in Cambridge during the working week. After his move to Cambridge, Lewis wrote less explicitly apologetic material. He now preferred to supplement his academic writings with more popular works – such as *Reflections on the Psalms* (1958) and *The Four Loves* (1960) – exploring aspects of the Christian faith for the benefit of believers.

Shortly after assuming his new position at Cambridge, Lewis married Joy Davidman, an American divorcée, in a civil ceremony in Oxford in April 1956. It was later discovered that Davidman had cancer. The death of his wife in 1960 prompted Lewis to write, under a pseudonym, *A Grief Observed*, now often cited as one of the finest accounts of the grieving process.

By June 1963, it was clear that Lewis's own health was failing. Long-standing problems placed his heart under strain. Lewis's doctors told him that there was no way of remedying his situation. Lewis accepted the inevitable, resigning from his Cambridge chair and discussing the possibility of his death openly with his friends and correspondents. He died at his Oxford home in the early evening of 22 November 1963, just hours before President John F. Kennedy died from gunshot wounds in Dallas, Texas. Lewis is buried in the churchyard of Holy Trinity Church, Headington Quarry, Oxford.

NOTES

1. The Grand Panorama: C.S. Lewis on the Meaning of Life

1. Jean-Paul Sartre, *Nausea* (New York: New Directions Publishing, 1964), 112.
2. Viktor E. Frankl, *Man's Search for Meaning* (New York: Simon and Schuster, 1963).
3. See Aaron Antonovsky, *Health, Stress and Coping* (San Francisco: Jossey-Bass Publishers, 1979).
4. See, for example, Irene Smith Landsman, 'Crises of Meaning in Trauma and Loss', in *Loss of the Assumptive World: A Theory of Traumatic Loss*, ed. Jeffrey Kauffman (New York: Brunner-Routledge, 2002), 13–30.
5. William James, *The Will to Believe* (New York: Dover Publications, 1956), 51.
6. Richard Dawkins, *River out of Eden: A Darwinian View of Life* (New York: Basic Books, 1995), 133.
7. C.S. Lewis, *Surprised by Joy* (London: HarperCollins, 2002), 198.
8. Ibid.
9. Ibid., 201.
10. Ibid., 197.

11. C.S. Lewis, 'The Poison of Subjectivism', in *Essay Collection and Other Short Pieces*, ed. Lesley Walmsley (London: HarperCollins, 2000), 250.

12. G.K. Chesterton, *The Everlasting Man* (San Francisco: Ignatius Press, 1993), 105.

13. C.S. Lewis, 'The Weight of Glory', in *Essay Collection*, 98.

14. 'Is Theology Poetry?', in *Essay Collection*, 21.

15. Dante Alighieri, *Paradiso*, XXXIII, 55–6.

16. G.K. Chesterton, 'The Return of the Angels', *Daily News*, 14 March 1903.

17. Ibid.

18. Ibid.

19. C.S. Lewis, *Mere Christianity* (New York: HarperOne, 2009), 136–7.

20. C.S. Lewis, *Allegory of Love* (London: Oxford University Press, 1936), 142.

21. C.S. Lewis, *The Discarded Image* (Cambridge: Cambridge University Press, 1994), 206.

22. Letter to L.T. Duff, 10 May 1943, in Barbara Reynolds (ed.), *The Letters of Dorothy L. Sayers: 1937 to 1943: From Novelist to Playwright*, vol. 2 (New York: St Martin's Press, 1996), 401.

23. Letter to the Archbishop of Canterbury, 7 September 1943, in Reynolds, *The Letters of Dorothy L. Sayers*, 429.

24. G.K. Chesterton, *Orthodoxy* (New York: John Lane Co., 1909), 293.

25. Lewis, 'The Weight of Glory', in *Essay Collection*, 105–6.

2. 'Old Friends to Trust': C.S. Lewis on Friendship

1. 'Get a Life!', *The Economist*, 17 August 2013, http://www.economist.com/news/science-and-technology/21583593-using-social-network-seems-make-people-more-miserable-get-life?fsrc=scn/fb/wl/pe/getalife.
2. Ray Pahl, *On Friendship* (Cambridge: Polity Press, 2000), 22.
3. C.S. Lewis, *The Four Loves* (London: HarperCollins, 2002), 80.
4. Ibid., 78.
5. Ibid., 78–9.
6. Lewis, *Surprised by Joy*, 151.
7. Walter Hooper (ed.), *The Collected Letters of C.S. Lewis,* vol. 1, *Family Letters 1905–1931* (San Francisco: HarperOne, 2004), 701.
8. Letter from Tolkien to Rayner Unwin, 12 September 1965, in Humphrey Carpenter (ed.), *The Letters of J.R.R. Tolkien* (London: HarperCollins, 1981), 362.
9. Colin Duriez, *C.S. Lewis: A Biography of Friendship* (Oxford: Lion Books, 2013), 79.
10. *The Four Loves*, 96.
11. Ibid., 99.
12. Bruce L. Edwards (ed.), *C.S. Lewis: Life, Works and Legacy*, 4 vols (Westport, CT: Praeger, 2007), 301.
13. 'The Inner Ring', in *Essay Collection*, 721–8.
14. Ibid., 724.

3. A Story-shaped World: C.S. Lewis on Narnia and the Importance of Stories

1. *Surprised by Joy*, 248.
2. 'The Weight of Glory', in *Essay Collection*, 99.
3. Ibid.
4. For a full discussion, see Alister E. McGrath, 'A Gleam of Divine Truth: The Concept of Myth in Lewis's Thought', in *The Intellectual World of C.S. Lewis* (Oxford: Wiley-Blackwell, 2013), 55–82.
5. J.R.R. Tolkien, 'On Fairy Stories', in *Tree and Leaf* (London: HarperCollins, 2001), 71.
6. Lewis to Roger Lancelyn Green, 28 December 1938, in *Letters*, vol. 2, 236–7.
7. The best study is David C. Downing, *Planets in Peril: A Critical Study of C.S. Lewis's Ransom Trilogy* (Amherst, MA: University of Massachusetts Press, 1992).
8. It's important to realise that Lewis had grasped the power of stories to challenge worldviews by the late 1930s. Some writers have suggested that Lewis turned to writing fiction as a result of a somewhat bruising encounter with the philosopher Elizabeth Anscombe in February 1948. But this has never been a persuasive argument. (For a discussion, see Alister E. McGrath, *C.S. Lewis – A Life: Eccentric Genius, Reluctant Prophet* [London: Hodder & Stoughton, 2013], 250–8.) Lewis had already written three works of science fiction and had mapped out some of the core themes of the Chronicles of Narnia before his encounter with Anscombe.

9. 'Sometimes Fairy Stories may say best what's to be said', in *Essay Collection*, 527.
10. 'It all began with a picture', in *Essay Collection*, 529. Lewis turned forty in November 1938.

4. The Lord and the Lion: C.S. Lewis on Aslan and the Christian Life

1. 'It all began with a picture', in *Essay Collection*, 529.
2. Letter to a fifth grade class in Maryland, 24 May 1954, in *Letters*, vol. 3, 480.
3. For a discussion of these views and their importance for Lewis's 'New Look', see Alister E. McGrath, 'The "New Look": Lewis's Philosophical Context at Oxford in the 1920s', in *The Intellectual World of C.S. Lewis*, 31–54.
4. For what follows, see *The Silver Chair*, 141–2.
5. For a detailed analysis, see Alister E. McGrath, 'Arrows of Joy: Lewis's Argument from Desire', in *The Intellectual World of C.S. Lewis*, 105–28.
6. *The Lion, the Witch and the Wardrobe*, 166.
7. Ibid., 65.
8. Letter to Arthur Greeves, 18 October 1931, in *Letters*, vol. 1, 977.
9. McGrath, *The Intellectual World of C.S. Lewis*, 68.
10. For the debate about the reading order of the Chronicles of Narnia, see McGrath, *C.S. Lewis – A Life*, 272–4.

11. Gilbert Meilander, *The Taste for the Other: The Social and Ethical Thought of C.S. Lewis* (Grand Rapids, MI: Eerdmans, 1978), 212–13.
12. Walter Hooper (ed.), *C.S. Lewis: A Complete Guide to His Life and Works* (London: HarperCollins, 1996), xi.
13. This great phrase comes from the excellent study of Louis Markos, *Restoring Beauty: The Good, the True, and the Beautiful in the Writings of C.S. Lewis* (Colorado Springs, CO: Biblica, 2010), 78–9.

5. Talking about Faith: C.S. Lewis on the Art of Apologetics

1. *Surprised by Joy*, 266.
2. Lewis to Miss Tunnicliff, 1 December 1951, in *Letters*, vol. 3, 146.
3. 'Christian Apologetics', in *Essay Collection*, 153.
4. Ibid., 155.
5. Austin Farrer, 'The Christian Apologist', in *Light on C.S. Lewis*, ed. Jocelyn Gibb (London: Geoffrey Bless, 1965), 37.
6. C. S. Lewis, *Mere Christianity* (London: Harper-Collins, 2002), 21.
7. Ibid., 8.
8. Ibid., 25.
9. Ibid., 137.
10. 'Is Theology Poetry?', in *Essay Collection*, 22.
11. Letter to Cecil Harwood, 28 October 1926, in Laurence Harwood, *C.S. Lewis, My Godfather: Letters, Photos and Recollections* (Downers Grove, IL: InterVarsity Press, 2007), 63.

12. Technically, this is known as the 'retrograde motion' of the planets, which arises when the earth overtakes the outer planets in the course of its annual orbit of the sun.
13. *Mere Christianity*, 29.
14. 'The Decline of Religion', in *Essay Collection*, 182.
15. Ibid.
16. Farrer, 'The Christian Apologist', 26. For comment on this assessment of Lewis, see John T. Stahl, 'Austin Farrer on C.S. Lewis as "The Christian Apologist"', *Christian Scholars' Review* 4 (1975): 231–7.
17. See Alister E. McGrath, 'Outside the "Inner Ring": Lewis as a Theologian', in *The Intellectual World of C.S. Lewis*, 163–83.
18. 'Christian Apologetics', in *Essay Collection*, 159. See also his letter to Mary van Deusen, 18 June 1956, in *Letters*, vol. 3, 762.

6. A Love of Learning: C.S. Lewis on Education

1. C.S. Lewis, *The Abolition of Man* (New York: HarperCollins, 2001), 29.
2. Ibid., 26.
3. A.N. Wilson, *C.S. Lewis: A Biography* (New York: W.W. Norton, 1990), 161.
4. Letter to Albert Lewis, 28 August 1924, in *Letters*, vol. 1, 633.
5. 'Henry Ford says "History is Bunk"', *New York Times*, 28 October 1921.

6. *Surprised by Joy*, 241.
7. 'On the Reading of Old Books', in *Essay Collection*, 439.
8. Ibid., 440.
9. 'Learning in War-Time', in *Essay Collection*, 584.
10. Ibid.
11. For the influence of this movement, see Angus McLaren, *Our Own Master Race: Eugenics in Canada 1885–1945* (Oxford: Oxford University Press, 1990); Pauline M.H. Mazumdar, *Eugenics, Human Genetics and Human Failings: The Eugenics Society, Its Sources and Its Critics in Britain* (London: Routledge, 1992); Richard Weikart, *From Darwin to Hitler: Evolutionary Ethics, Eugenics, and Racism in Germany* (New York: Palgrave Macmillan, 2004).
12. For the story of this bizarre idea, see John S. Partington, 'H.G. Wells's Eugenic Thinking of the 1930s and 1940s', *Utopian Studies* 14, no. 1 (2003): 74–81. See also John Gray, *The Immortalization Commission: Science and the Strange Quest to Cheat Death* (New York: Farrar, Straus and Giroux, 2011).
13. C.S. Lewis, *An Experiment in Criticism* (Cambridge: Cambridge University Press, 1992), 140–1.
14. Ibid., 137.
15. Ibid., 85.
16. *Surprised by Joy*, 221–2.
17. '*De audiendis Poetis*', in *Studies in Medieval and Renaissance Literature* (Cambridge: Cambridge University Press, 2007), 2–3.

18. Letter to the *Church Times*, 8 February 1952, in C.S. Lewis, *Collected Letters*, ed. Walter Hooper, vol. 3 (San Francisco: HarperOne, 2007), 164.
19. 'On the Reading of Old Books', in *Essay Collection*, 439.
20. Ibid.
21. Ibid., 440.

7. Coping with Suffering: C.S. Lewis on the Problem of Pain

1. *The Magician's Nephew*, 166.
2. *Surprised by Joy*, 227.
3. *The Problem of Pain*, 91.
4. Ibid.
5. Ibid., xii.
6. Ibid., 3.
7. Ibid., 25.
8. Ibid., 16.
9. Ibid., 94.
10. Ibid., 33–9.
11. Ibid., 39.
12. Ibid., 80.
13. Ibid., 148–59.
14. Ibid., 153.
15. Katharine Farrer (1911–72) authored the 'Inspector Ringwood' trilogy (1952–7).
16. For Farrer's own approach to evil and suffering, see Austin Farrer, *Love Almighty and Ills Unlimited* (London: Collins, 1966).

17. For the full story, see McGrath, *C. S. Lewis – A Life*, 320–47.
18. C.S. Lewis, *A Grief Observed* (New York: HarperCollins, 1994), 5–6.
19. Ibid., 52.
20. Ibid., 44.
21. Ibid.
22. Austin Farrer, 'In His Image: In Commemoration of C.S. Lewis', in Charles C. Conti (ed.), *The Brink of Mystery* (London: SPCK, 1976), 45–7.

8. *'Further up and Further in': C.S. Lewis on Hope and Heaven*

1. *Mere Christianity*, 136–7.
2. Ibid., 134.
3. Cyprian of Carthage, *On Mortality*, 7. Cyprian was martyred for his faith in 258 during the Decian persecution.
4. John Donne, *The Works of John Donne*, ed. Henry Alford, vol. 3 (London: Parker, 1839), 574–5.
5. Letter to Arthur Greeves, 27 June 1961, in *Letters*, vol. 3, 1, 277.
6. Letter to Cecil Harwood, 29 August 1963, in *Letters*, vol. 3, 1, 452.
7. Letter to Mary Willis Shelburne, 28 June 1963, in *Letters*, vol. 3, 1, 434.
8. *Surprised by Joy*, 245.
9. For a full discussion of this period in Lewis's life, see McGrath, 'The "New Look"', 31–54.

10. For example, see Andrew Walker, 'Scripture, Revelation and Platonism in C.S. Lewis', *Scottish Journal of Theology* 55 (2002): 19–35.
11. *The Last Battle*, 160.
12. Ibid., 159.
13. *Miracles*, 256.
14. *The Last Battle*, 161.
15. 'The Weight of Glory', in *Essay Collection*, 99.
16. *Mere Christianity*, 134.
17. Ibid., 137.
18. *The Last Battle*, 172.
19. 'The Weight of Glory', in *Essay Collection*, 102.

ABOUT THE AUTHOR

A lister McGrath is a best-selling author of more than fifty books and a popular speaker, travelling the world every year to speak at various conferences. He is Professor of Theology, Ministry and Education at King's College, London, and head of its Centre for Theology, Religion and Culture. He is currently Senior Research Fellow at Harris Manchester College at Oxford University and President of the Oxford Centre for Christian Apologetics. Before moving to King's College, Dr McGrath was Professor of Historical Theology at Oxford University. After initial academic work in the natural sciences, McGrath turned to the study of theology and intellectual history, while occasionally becoming engaged in broader cultural debates about the rationality and relevance of the Christian faith. He has a long-standing interest in educational issues, and has developed a series of theological textbooks which are widely used throughout the world.

Like Lewis, McGrath was born in Belfast and became an atheist as a young man, before rediscovering the Christian faith at Oxford University. McGrath's deep knowledge of Christian theology, history and literature allows him to interpret Lewis against a broad backdrop, presenting a fascinating portrait of the development of Lewis's mind and his impact on Western culture.